THE COLOSSEUM

THE COLOSSEUM

KEITH HOPKINS

AND

MARY BEARD

HARVARD UNIVERSITY PRESS
Cambridge, Massachusetts
2005

Copyright © 2005 by Keith Hopkins and Mary Beard
First published in Great Britain in 2005 by

Profile Books Ltd
58A Hatton Garden
London ECIN 8LX

Library of Congress Cataloging-in-Publication Data

Hopkins, Keith, 1934–
The Colosseum / Keith Hopkins and Mary Beard
p. cm. — (Wonders of the world)
Includes bibliographical references and index.
ISBN 0-674-01895-8 (alk. paper)
1. Colosseum (Rome, Italy) 2. Amphitheaters—Rome.
3. Rome (Italy)—Buildings, structures, etc. 4. Rome (Italy)—Antiquities.
I. Beard, Mary, 1955– II. Title. III. Wonders of the world (Cambridge, Mass.)

DG68.1.H67 2005   937′.6—dc22   2005046011

Printed in the United Kingdom
by Butler and Tanner

CONTENTS

PREFACE

The Colosseum is the most famous, and instantly recognisable, monument to have survived from the classical world. So famous, in fact, that for over seventy years, from 1928 to 2000, a fragment of its distinctive colonnade was displayed on the medals awarded to victorious athletes at the Olympic Games – as a symbol of classicism and of the modern Games' ancient ancestor.

It was not until the Sydney Games in 2000 that this caused any controversy. British newspapers – most of which did not know that the Colosseum had been gracing Olympic medals for more than half a century – enjoyed poking fun at the ignorance of the antipodeans who apparently had not grasped the simple fact that the Colosseum was Roman and the Games were Greek. The Australian–Greek press took a loftier tone; as one Greek editor thundered, 'The Colosseum is a stadium of blood. It has nothing to do with the Olympic ideals of peace and brotherhood.'

The International Olympic Committee wriggled slightly, but stood their ground. They had already prevented the organisers of the Games replacing the Colosseum with the profile of the Sydney Opera House, so they presumably had their arguments ready. The design, they insisted, was traditional and it was not, in any case, the Roman Colosseum

1. The Sydney Olympic medal (2000) displays the distinctive form of the Colosseum behind the Goddess of Victory and a racing chariot. 'The Ultimate Ignorance' complained one Greek newspaper in Australia.

specifically, but rather a 'generic' Colosseum: 'As far as we are concerned, it's not important if it's the Colosseum or the Parthenon. What's important is that it's a stadium.'

Unsurprisingly, the Colosseum motif had been replaced by the time the Games went (back) to Greece in 2004. The ponderously titled 'Committee to Change the Design of the Olympic Medal' came up with a new, Greek and much less instantly recognisable design: a figure of Victory flying over the Panathinaikon stadium built in Athens to host the first modern Games in 1896. But the questions that this argument raised about the Colosseum itself still remain. What was its original purpose? (Certainly not the racing signalled by the miniature chariot also depicted on the medal.) How should we now respond to the bloody combats of gladiators that have come to define its image in modern culture? Why is it such a famous monument?

These are just some of the questions we set out to answer in this book.

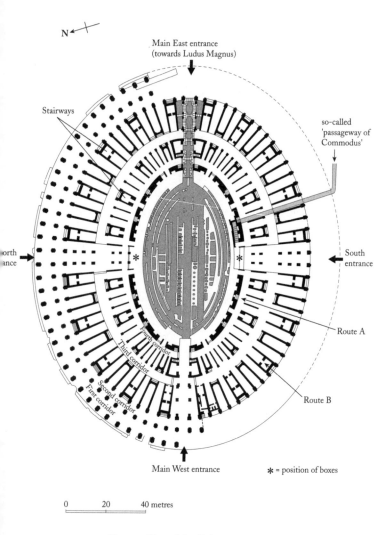

N

Main East entrance
(towards Ludus Magnus)

Stairways

so-called
'passageway of
Commodus'

North
entrance

South
entrance

Route A

Fourth corridor
Third corridor
Second corridor
First corridor

Route B

Main West entrance   ✱ = position of boxes

0   20   40 metres

Figure 1. Plan of the Colosseum.

[x]

THE COLOSSEUM NOW ...

COLOSSEUM BY MOONLIGHT

In 1843 the first edition of *Murray's Handbook to Central Italy*, the essential pocketbook companion for the well-heeled Victorian tourist, enthusiastically recommended a visit to the Colosseum (or the 'Coliseum' as it was then regularly spelled). Many aspects of Rome, it warned, would prove inconvenient or disappointing. The Roman system of time-keeping was simply baffling for the punctual British visitor; its twenty-four-hour clock began an hour and a half after sunset, so times changed with the seasons. The local cuisine left a lot to be desired ('A good restaurateur is still one of the *desiderata* of Rome', moaned the *Handbook*, somewhat sniffily). Accommodation too could be difficult to find, especially for those with special requirements – the invalids who were recommended to search out rooms with 'a southern aspect', or the 'nervous persons' advised to 'live in more open and elevated situations'. Yet the Colosseum was guaranteed not to disappoint. In fact, it was even more impressive in real life than its reputation might suggest: 'There is no monument of ancient Rome which artists and engravers have made so familiar to readers of all classes ... and there is certainly none of which the descriptions and drawings are so far surpassed by the reality.' No need then to promote its virtues or guide the visitor's response. 'We shall not attempt to anticipate the feelings of the traveller,' the *Handbook* continued, 'or obtrude upon him a single word which may interfere with his own impressions, but simply supply him with such facts as may be useful in his examination of the ruin.'

A brisk account followed, with plenty of dry dates, dimensions and figures. Building work started under the emperor Vespasian in AD 72, with the opening ceremonies under his son Titus in 80; the last recorded wild beast show in the arena took place in the reign of Theodoric (who died in AD 526) – unless you count a bull-fight staged in 1332. The whole structure covered some 6 acres and was built of travertine stone (mixed with brick in the interior). Its outer elevation comprised four storeys, to a total of 157 English feet, with eighty arches on the ground floor giving an entrance to seats and arena. Inside, the arena measured 278 by 177 feet and was originally surrounded by seating in four separate tiers which could accommodate, according to one late Roman description, 87,000 spectators. And so on. But, in traditional guidebook style, the pill of these facts and figures was sugared by the occasional curious myth, anecdote or arcane piece of knowledge. Hence the reference to a story put about by the Church, in a fit of wishful thinking, that the architect of the Colosseum had actually been a Christian and a martyr by the name of Gaudentius; and hence the account of the plans of Pope Sixtus V in the sixteenth century to convert the whole building into a wool factory, with shops in the arcades – a scheme which, even though abandoned, came at enormous financial cost to the pontiff. There were also misconceptions to be corrected. Those puzzling little holes all over the building were not, as many people had said, where poles had been inserted to support the booths erected for the medieval fairs that took place there. They were instead (and this is still thought to be the correct explanation) where enterprising medieval hucksters had dug into the structure to remove and make off with the iron clamps which held the blocks together.

Helpful hints were offered too on how to make the most of a visit. The important thing, then as now, was to get as high up on the building as possible. For the Victorian visitor, a special staircase had been constructed to give access to the upper storeys 'and thence as high as the parapet'. From here, where there was a view both into the Colosseum itself and out over such notable antiquities as the Arch of Constantine, the Palatine Hill and the Roman Forum, 'the scene … is one of the most impressive in the world'. If this might seem perilously close to an 'attempt to anticipate the feelings of the traveller', then even more so was the insistence that the view was best at night, by the light of the moon. 'There are few travellers who do not visit this spot by moonlight in order to realise the magnificent description in "Manfred", the only description which has ever done justice to the wonders of the Coliseum.' As if to underline the point, and to tell the visitor exactly how to react, a substantial chunk of Lord Byron's 'Manfred' was quoted, with its famous comparison of the night-time impact of the standing – albeit ruined – Colosseum ('the gladiators' bloody Circus') and the paltry and overgrown remains of what had once been the palace of the Roman emperors ('Caesar's chambers, and the Augustan halls') on the Palatine:

I do remember me, that in my youth,
When I was wandering, – upon such a night
I stood within the Coloseum's wall,
Midst the chief relics of almighty Rome;

...

... Where the Caesars dwelt,
And dwell the tuneless birds of night, amidst
A grove which springs through levell'd battlements,
And twines its roots with the imperial hearths,
Ivy usurps the laurel's place of growth; –
But the gladiators' bloody Circus stands,
A noble wreck in ruinous perfection!
While Caesar's chambers, and the Augustan halls,
Grovel on earth in indistinct decay. –
And thou didst shine, thou rolling moon, upon
All this, and cast a wide and tender light,
Which soften'd down the hoar austerity
Of rugged desolation, and fill'd up,
As 'twere anew, the gaps of centuries.

Thanks in part, no doubt, to their appearance in the *Handbook*, these lines became one the most influential ways of 'seeing' the Colosseum, and were dramatically declaimed, or repeated *sotto voce*, by countless Victorian (and later) visitors to the monument.

For the rest of the nineteenth century, succeeding editions of *Murray's Handbook* continued to insist that moonlight was the prime time to appreciate the Colosseum and to give detailed instructions on whether special permission was needed and, if so, how to obtain it. By 1862 an even more atmospheric option was available for the most plutocratic of tourists, a private light show: 'The lighting-up of the Coliseum with blue and red lights, a splendid sight, can be effected, having previously obtained the permission of the police, at an expense of about 150 scudi, everything included.' One would hope that it *was* 'all inclusive'; at the rate of exchange with the pound advertised in the *Handbook*, 150 scudi is not far short of an adult manual worker's annual wage in England at the time. No surprise perhaps that, after Rome became capital of the united Italy in 1870, such an extravaganza was taken over by the public authorities. The 1881 edition of the *Handbook* advised that the 'illumination of the Colosseum with white, green and red lights, a splendid sight, takes place generally once a year, on the *Natale di Roma* (21 April), or on the occasion of some royal persons visiting the Eternal City.' Even if the moon failed, in other words, the Birthday of Rome would always offer a dramatically floodlit Colosseum.

ROMAN FEVER

Yet scratch the surface of this apparently up-beat image of nineteenth-century tourism to the Colosseum and some rather more uncomfortable aspects emerge. This was partly a question of Protestant anxieties about the Catholic 'take-over' of the monument. A cross in the middle of the arena and a series of shrines at the edges were one thing – appropriate commemoration of the Christian martyrs who had supposedly lost their lives there. The idea that, as the *Handbook* had it, kissing the cross bought 'an indulgence of 200 days' was quite another. Equally awkward (even if it offered a picturesque vignette of primitive piety) was the

Roma - Interno del Colosseo

2. A memento of the Colosseum. This mid-nineteenth-century tourist postcard shows the shrines of the Stations of the Cross around the edge of the arena and (in shadow) the central cross.

'rude pulpit' near by, from where a monk preached every Friday. The best you could say was that it was 'impossible not to be impressed with the solemnity of a Christian service in a scene so much identified with the early history of our common faith' (though, even then, the phrase 'our common faith' must have been a hard-working euphemism).

There was also, predictably, the question of how far the romantic image of the lonely Colosseum by moonlight, so heavily advertised by the *Handbook* and other guides, was a self-defeating piece of propaganda. The impression we get elsewhere is that the Colosseum by night could be, by nineteenth-century standards at least, far too crowded and far too un-romantic for comfort. For example, in Nathaniel Hawthorne's novel *The Marble Faun* (1860), set among a group of expatriate artists in Rome, a moonlit visit to the monument involves negotiating a host of other visitors, laughing and shrieking, flirting and playing peek-a-boo among the shadowy arcades. Hawthorne paints a vivid picture of mindless tourism. One party was singing (drunkenly, we are meant to imagine) on the steps of the central cross; another, English or American, following the instructions of the *Handbook* to the letter and 'paying the inevitable visit by moonlight', had climbed up to the parapet and were 'exalting themselves with raptures that were Byron's not their own'. No chance for silent contemplation of the wonders here.

At the same time, though, it was possible to feel frustrated that in some respects the commercial possibilities of the monument had not been sufficiently realised. One of the glories of the Colosseum, until it was aggressively weeded and tidied up in 1871, was the vast range of flower species that had colonised its nooks and crannies – well over 400 different types, according to the most systematic study (illustration 30, p. 179). Why on earth, wondered the *Handbook* in 1843, was not more done with these? 'With such materials for a *hortus siccus* [a collection of dried flowers], it is surprising that the Romans do not make complete collections for sale, on the plan of the Swiss herbaria; we cannot imagine any memorial of the Coliseum which would be more acceptable to the traveller.'

But all these were side-issues compared with the central problem that faced any visitor who knew something of the history of the building. How could one reconcile the magnificence of the structure, the scale and impact of what remained, with its original function and the memories of bloody gladiatorial combat and Christian martyrdom that had taken place in its arena? The *Handbook* skirted the problem briefly but awkwardly – and without even pointing explicitly to the *human* carnage that had been wreaked in the Colosseum: 'The gladiatorial spectacles of which it was the scene for nearly 400 years are matters of history, and it is not necessary to dwell upon them further than to state that at the dedication of the building by Titus, 5000 wild beasts were slain in the arena, and the games in honour of the event lasted for nearly 100 days.'

Many others in the nineteenth century, however, visitors and writers alike, did feel a need to dwell on what had happened there and to debate the effect it must have on their appreciation of the monument. It is a theme that underlies Byron's verses quoted earlier (how come that this monument of cruelty survives when the imperial palace has left such paltry traces?) and it was harped on too by Charles Dickens when he visited Italy in the 1840s ('Never, in its bloodiest prime, can the sight of the gigantic Coliseum … have moved one heart as it must move all who look upon it now, a ruin. God be thanked: a ruin!'). But the debate is perhaps most sharply dramatised in Madame de Staël's novel *Corinne*, when the exotic poetess who is the heroine of the book takes her Scottish admirer Lord Oswald Nelvil on a guided tour of the sights of Rome. The highlight of the day was the Colosseum, 'the most beautiful ruin in Rome', Corinne enthused. But Oswald (who was, frankly, rather a prig) 'did not allow himself to share Corinne's admiration. As he looked at the four galleries, the four structures, rising one above the other, at the mixture of pomp and decay which simultaneously arouses respect and pity, he could only see the masters' luxury and the slaves' blood.' Despite her spirited defence of her position, Corinne signally failed to convince him that it was possible to appreciate the magnificence of the architecture separately from any disgust for the immoral purpose it had once served. 'He was looking for a moral feeling everywhere and all the magic of the arts could never satisfy him'; nor in the end could the magic of Corinne.

In fact, the Colosseum repeatedly appears in nineteenth-century literature as a site of tragedy and an emblem of death, both ancient and modern. For memories of the slaughter of gladiators went hand in hand with the belief that the damp and chill evening air of the monument – romantic moonlit vista though it may have been – was a particularly virulent carrier of the potentially fatal malarial 'Roman fever'. (This notorious danger of the Roman air is discussed in detail by the *Handbook*, in a section – significantly – placed directly after the description of the Protestant cemetery.) It was Roman fever that carried off Henry James' Daisy Miller after she had flouted social convention to spend the evening in the Colosseum alone with her Italian admirer, Signor Giovanelli. 'Well, I *have* seen the Colosseum by moonlight … That's one good thing' she shouted defiantly, in what were almost her last words, to her other admirer, and critic, the ineffectual Mr Winterbourne (who was also lurking in the Colosseum, where he had been murmuring – what else? – 'Byron's famous lines out of *Manfred*'). The moonlit Colosseum proves only slightly less treacherous in Edith Wharton's brilliantly satirical short story from the 1930s, 'Roman Fever', which exposes the shady past of two middle-aged American matrons – Mrs Slade and Mrs Ansley – who are spending the afternoon together in a restaurant close to the Colosseum. In little more than a dozen pages, it comes to light that, years earlier, just before their respective marriages, Mrs Slade, suspicious of her fiancé's interest in the other woman, had tricked Mrs Ansley into spending a perilous evening in the Colosseum. She had caught a nasty chill there, it is true. But, more to the point, as is revealed in the last line, she had also conceived her lovely daughter Barbara in its shadows – by Mr Slade. The Colosseum's association with death and flirtation is here neatly rolled into one.

There were, however, other ways of discussing the gloomy or violent side of the monument. The hyperbole of Byron, Dickens and the like in conjuring the romantic image of a place of cruelty, sadness and transgression was hilariously subverted by Mark Twain in his 1860s tale of European travel, *Innocents Abroad* – a book which in his lifetime sold many more copies than *Tom Sawyer* or *Huckleberry Finn*. In some ways Twain was as enthusiastic an admirer of the

Colosseum as anyone, dubbing it 'the monarch of all European ruins' and much enjoying the irony of seeing 'lizards sun themselves in the sacred seat of the Emperor'. But his best joke was to pretend to have found in Rome a surviving ancient playbill for a gladiatorial show, as well as a review of the proceedings from *The Roman Daily Battle-Ax.* Both, unsurprisingly, were almost identical in style and tone to their late nineteenth-century Broadway equivalents. Top of the bill was 'MARCUS MARCELLUS VALERIAN! FOR SIX NIGHTS ONLY!!' followed by 'a GALAXY OF TALENT! such as has not been beheld in Rome before … The performance will commence this evening with a GRAND BROADSWORD COMBAT! between two young and promising amateurs and a celebrated Parthian gladiator … The whole to conclude with a chaste and elegant GENERAL SLAUGHTER!' The spoof review chimed in nicely:

The opening scene last night … was very fine. The elder of the two young gentlemen handled his weapon with a grace that marked the possession of extraordinary talent. His feint of thrusting, followed instantly by a happily delivered blow which unhelmeted the Parthian, was received with hearty applause. He was not thoroughly up in the backhanded stroke, but it was very gratifying to his numerous friends to know that, in time, practice would have overcome this defect. However he was killed. His sisters, who were present, expressed considerable regret. His mother left the Coliseum … The general slaughter was rendered with a faithfulness to detail which reflects the highest credit upon the late participants in it.

It is not hard to see what kind of high emotional writing about the Colosseum and its gladiatorial games Twain had in his sights. Indeed he proudly declared that he was 'the only free white man of mature age' who had written about the monument since Byron without quoting that other Byronic catch-phrase on the Colosseum's victims (this time from *Childe Harold's Pilgrimage*) – 'butchered to make a Roman holiday'. It 'sounds well', he explained, 'for the first seventeen or eighteen thousand times one sees it in print, but after that it begins to grow tiresome'. Twain obviously had a point. But changing the rhetoric of response does not make the problem go away. His own humorous modernising, his domestication of the gladiatorial games into modern Broadway entertainment, was in the end another way of emphasising the main dilemma of the nineteenth-century visitor: how to make sense of the murderous games that had once taken place within the magnificent walls of the Colosseum. Was it really like Broadway? Of course not.

COLOSSEUM TODAY

The experience of early twenty-first-century tourists is both like and unlike that of their counterparts of a hundred and fifty years ago. There is now no regular moonlight access for even the wealthy visitor, still less is there any chance of private floodlighting on request. A modernist lift has replaced the old staircase giving access to the upper floors, but it is no longer possible to climb to the very topmost level of the building. Today's tourists must make do with what is still a fabulous view, but from short of half the way up. The Christian additions have also been down-played. Gone is the dominant central cross, indulgences and the Friday sermon; though a cross does remain to one side of the arena (placed there under the Fascist regime in 1926 – illustration 29, p. 176), the Pope still visits every year to perform the rituals of Good Friday and the continued insistence on the stories of Christian martyrdom makes the building a powerful point of intersection between the modern religious world and the ancient. There is even less peace and quiet now than there ever was. If a moonlit walk through the arena was a popular pastime in the nineteenth century, the numbers involved certainly did not match the almost 3 million people who currently visit each year. And they are served by a tourist industry which may not offer the dried flowers that the *Handbook* considered such an appropriate souvenir of the Colosseum, but which does provide mementoes of the monument in almost every other conceivable form – from illuminated plastic to candy and fridge-magnets.

One way of seeing the changes over the last century or so is as a shift from romantic ruin to archaeological site. Some of the building's impact has remained more or less the same through that transition. There are very few visitors who have failed to be struck by the vast size of the Colosseum. (Ironically the man to whom the building owes a good deal of its fame in modern popular culture, Ridley Scott, the director of *Gladiator*, is one of the handful to remain unimpressed; he is said to have found the actual building rather 'small' and to have preferred a mock-up built in Malta and digitally enhanced.) But the rigorous cleaning of the surviving remains, the removal of plants and flowers and the exposure of the complicated foundations and substructures have all combined not only to preserve the building and to yield all

[13]

3. Lighting up. The Colosseum ablaze 12–13 December, 1999 to celebrate the abolition of the death penalty in Albania.

sorts of new technical information about its construction and chronology; they have also made the Colosseum seem, to all but the most specialist of visitors, more desolate, more baffling in its layout and considerably more difficult to navigate.

Any visitor will almost certainly be amazed by the overpowering bulk of the outside walls; but when they cross the threshold, (queue up to) buy a ticket and peek into the arena, they are confronted by what is likely to seem at best a confusing mass of masonry, at worst a jumble of dilapidated stone and rubble. After all, the reason that moonlit strolls around the arena are no longer possible is not simply the more conservative opening hours of the modern state-controlled site. It is also because there is hardly any surface of the arena to walk on. What was left at the centre of the Colosseum after the archaeological work of the late nineteenth and early twentieth century is a maze of foundation walls and industrial supports for the machinery that would have brought up the animals into the arena to face the waiting crowd. Gone is the earth that once covered all this, and allowed the Victorian traveller to wander at will. In its place, and only recently installed (for most of the twentieth century the centre of the Colosseum was a gaping hole), is a small section of wooden flooring – on the model of what is believed was the Roman original. Not only is this no place for flirtation, still less conception; it is also very difficult for the mind's eye to flesh out the brutal skeleton of the building now on display, and to recapture a living environment from its dead and battered frame. It is predictable perhaps that an elderly Italian architect should recently have come up with a scheme for forgetting about the ruin and simply rebuilding the whole lot, as new. ('It would be a good thing for someone like Coca-Cola to fund …' he suggested. 'They could tell the whole world that they had completed the Colosseum.')

For all these differences, however, the old problem of how to react to a monument with such a bloodstained history remains. In fact, even more than it was a century and a half ago, the Colosseum has become for us the defining symbol of ancient Rome precisely *because of* (not despite) the fact that it raises so many of the questions and dilemmas that we face in any engagement with Roman culture. How different was their society from our own? What judgements of it are we entitled to make? Can we admire the magnificence and the technical accomplishments, while simultaneously deploring the cruelty and the violence? How far are we taking vicarious pleasure in the excesses of Roman luxury or bloodlust, at the same time as we lament them? Are some societies really more violent than others?

All modern responses to the Colosseum – this book inevitably included – turn out to be a combination of admiration, repulsion and a measure of insidious smugness. For it *is* an extraordinarily bravura feat of architecture and a marker of the indelibility of ancient Rome from the modern landscape, yet the scale of the human slaughter in the arena must revolt us, while simultaneously allowing us to take comfort in the belief that 'our' culture is not like that. Modern responses also tend to be a mixture of horror at the alien past and a cosy domestication of its strangeness, a convenient translation of their world into ours.

This translation takes various forms. It was the game played by Mark Twain as long ago as the 1860s when he burst the romantic bubble by rewriting the gladiatorial shows as

Broadway theatre. Twain would no doubt have been pleased to know that the modern city authorities in Rome have actually used the Colosseum again as an 'entertainment' venue. In 2003 Paul McCartney played a charity concert inside the arena to a select audience of 400 who were paying up to £1000 a head for their tickets – before going on to give a more democratic, free show to 300,000 people outside the monument's walls. 'I think we're the first band to play here since the Christians,' he quipped. (Not quite: an acoustically disastrous concert had been staged in the arena by Rome's opera company in 1951 to celebrate the fiftieth anniversary of the death of the composer Verdi).

But domestication is also what drives the lively tourist industry that has grown up on the pavements outside the Colosseum, where – for a price – visitors can have their photographs taken with burly young Italians dressed up as gladiators-cum-Roman-centurions. So intense was this trade that a few years ago a turf war broke out among the 'gladiators' fighting for the best pitches and, as a result, they must now be licensed (up to a maximum of fifty, no criminal records and plastic weapons only). But, street fighting and profiteering apart, the message is clear. Ancient gladiators were friendly kinds of guys; and, if they were with us today, they too would be phoning up their girlfriends on their mobiles between photos, or snatching a cigarette and a Peroni in the local bar. Or, alternatively, they would be snatching a Pepsi, as a notable television commercial recently tried to convince us. Rumoured to be the most expensive advertisement ever made, it featured Britney Spears, Beyoncé Knowles and a number of other A-list pop stars as female gladiators in the Colosseum who – thanks to the

4. Outside the Colosseum. Modern gladiators lure unwary tourists into an embarrassing holiday photograph.

reverberations produced by their rousing chorus of 'We will rock you' – manage to open up the emperor's private Pepsi supplies and provide free drinks for all.

Yet the domestication is never complete, and these attempts at translation always leave much rougher edges than the comfortable image of the modern lookalikes, with their mobile phones and fizzy drinks, might suggest. The Colosseum's tantalising appeal still depends, in part, on the frisson that comes with the blood and the violence. It is this combination of the dangerous and the safe, of the funny and the frankly revolting, that accounts for its power in popular culture and the thrill (crowds, heat and a confusing mass of masonry notwithstanding) of a visit. There is still a sense of transgression in the paradox of taking pleasure in touring the site where Romans took their pleasure in state-sponsored mass murder; and – for the more reflective at least – in wondering quite where the similarities between the Romans and ourselves start, or stop.

It is hardly surprising that this power has been harnessed (and re-invigorated) by some of the biggest business interests in the world. It may finally come as a relief to know that it has also been harnessed by some more noble causes. One of the most moving recent developments in the long history of the 'Colosseum by night' is the floodlighting campaign launched in 1999, with the support of, among others, the Pope, Amnesty International and the Rome city council. With the slogan 'The Colosseum lights up life', the building is bathed in golden light each time a death sentence is commuted anywhere in the world, or when any state votes to suspend or abolish its use (illustration 3). It is a clever piece of propaganda and of re-appropriation. 'I think all over the world the Colosseum is known as a place of death,' explained the mayor of Rome. 'Today we want to make a positive link between the Colosseum and life.' Or, as the Egyptian news agency Al-Ahram put it more bluntly (unencumbered by the romantic image of the monument that still haunts most in the West), 'This noxious landmark … this ancient killing ground has become a symbol of life and mercy.'

2

... AND THEN

'ALL WORKS TO CAESAR'S THEATRE GIVE PLACE'

'The Amphitheatre' or 'Hunting Theatre', as it was then called ('Colosseum' or 'Coliseum' is the medieval sobriquet which has stuck), was no less renowned in the ancient world than it has become in the modern. We should not fall into the trap of imagining that Roman reactions to the building were anything like identical to ours. Some Romans would certainly have shared our ambivalence towards a monument constructed for the enjoyment of murder – in increasing numbers, as Christianity became a major religion in the ancient world; but that cannot have been the orthodox view among the inhabitants of Rome in the first two centuries AD. It is also the case that the Romans themselves had many other monuments to choose from if they wanted to select a building to symbolise their capital city and its culture. For us, the Colosseum is one of the few remains well enough pre-served to make a powerful and memorable icon of ancient Rome (the columns of Trajan and Marcus Aurelius and the Pantheon are probably its only rivals). The Romans would have been spoiled for choice. The great temple of Jupiter on the Capitoline Hill or the vast complex of halls, shops and libraries known as Trajan's Forum (the column was originally its centrepiece) would both have seemed more than equal to

5. The classic image of the Colosseum, immortalised on countless postcards, souvenirs – and as the design on the modern Italian five cent coin.

the Colosseum in magnificence and wealth of symbolic associations, while the great venue for chariot racing, the Circus Maximus, although today a deeply disappointing patch of grass, once held some 250,000 spectators, several times the capacity of the Colosseum.

Nonetheless, those archaeologists who rather loftily suggest that the fame of the Colosseum is a modern invention – a result of our own obsessions and not much to do with the Romans – must be wrong. Or at least they fly in the face of a good deal of evidence for the monument's ancient renown. The most extravagant example of this is the slim book of verse specially composed by the Roman poet Martial to celebrate the inaugural games in the Colosseum, where no hype is spared in praising the building. The opening poem explicitly ranks it ahead of an international, and partly mythical, roster of ancient Wonders of the World: the pyramids, the city walls of Babylon, the temple of Diana at Ephesus, the altar made by the god Apollo on the island of Delos (from horns of deer that his sister Artemis had killed) and the tomb of Mausolus at Halicarnassus. To quote Henry Killigrew's jaunty seventeenth-century translation:

> *Egypt*, forbear thy Pyramids to praise,
> A barb'rous Work up to a Wonder raise;
> Let *Babylon* cease th'incessant Toyl to prize,
> Which made her Walls to such immensness rise!
> Nor let th'*Ephesians* boast the curious Art,
> Which Wonder to their Temple does impart.
> *Delos* dissemble too the high Renown,
> Which did thy Horn-fram'd Altar lately crown;
> *Caria* to vaunt thy Mausoleum spare,

Sumptuous for Cost, and yet for Art more rare,
As not borne up, but pendulous i'th'Air:
All Works to *Caesar*'s Theatre give place,
This Wonder *Fame* above the rest does grace.

Of course, Martial was not an impartial witness. As the in-house poet of the imperial court, one might argue, it was his job not simply to reflect the fame of the monument but to use his art to *make it famous*. If so, then he was strikingly successful, as a vivid account (by the late-Roman historian Ammianus Marcellinus) of the visit of the emperor Constantius II to Rome in AD 357 suggests. Constantius had been emperor for twenty years but had never actually been to the capital before; most of his reign had been spent dealing with the Persians in the East and with rivals to his throne in other parts of the empire. Combining public business with some energetic sightseeing around the attractions of the city, he is said to have been very struck by the 'huge bulk of the amphitheatre'. True, there were other monuments also reported to have caught his attention, and pride of place seems to have gone to Trajan's Forum, where he stood 'transfixed with astonishment'. But the Colosseum was not far behind, a building so tall that 'the human eye can hardly reach its highest point'.

It was not just a matter of literary fame, however. Perhaps the clearest indication of the monument's importance in the Roman world is the rash of imitations it spawned. Although there were several earlier stone amphitheatres, once the Colosseum had been built it seems to have become the model for many, if not most, of those that followed, both in Italy and in the provinces – well over two hundred by the end

[24]

of the second century AD on current estimates. The façade of the Capua amphitheatre in southern Italy, for example, which seems to have had a succession of columns in the different architectural orders – Tuscan, Ionic and Corinthian – immediately evokes its predecessor in Rome. Further afield, the third-century amphitheatre at El Jem in modern Tunisia (which still dominates its modern town almost as dramatically as does the Colosseum) seems to have been designed so closely on the pattern of the Roman example as to be in effect 'a shrunken Colosseum'. Exactly how the design was copied or what technical processes of architectural imitation were involved, we do not know. But somehow the Colosseum became an almost instant archetype, a marker of 'Romanness' across the empire.

A variety of factors combined to give the Colosseum this iconic status in ancient Rome. As the reaction of Constantius implies, size was certainly important. It was, by a considerable margin, the biggest amphitheatre in the empire; in fact some of the more modest structures, such as those at Chester or Caerleon in Britain, would have fitted comfortably into the space of the Colosseum's central arena. But size was not everything. The strong association of both the form and function of the building with specifically *Roman* culture also played a part. Many individual elements of the design certainly derived from Greek architectural precedents, but the form as a whole was, unusually, something distinctively Roman – as were the activities that went on within it (even if gladiatorial spectacles were later enthusiastically taken up in the Greek world). A key factor too was the role of the Colosseum in Roman history and politics. For it not only signalled the pleasures of popular entertainment, it also symbolised a particular style of interaction between the Roman emperor and the people of Rome. It stood at the very heart of the delicate balance between Roman autocracy and popular power, an object lesson in Roman imperial statecraft. This is clear from the very moment of its foundation: its origins are embedded in an exemplary tale of dynastic change, imperial transgression, and competition for control of the city of Rome itself.

'ROME'S TO IT SELF RESTOR'D'

The history of the Colosseum goes back to the year AD 68, when after a flamboyant reign the emperor Nero committed suicide. The senate had passed the ancient equivalent of a vote of no confidence, his staff and bodyguards were rapidly deserting him. So the emperor made for the out-of-town villa of one of his remaining servants and (with a little help) stabbed himself in the throat – reputedly uttering his famous boast, 'What an artist dies in me!' ('*Qualis artifex pereo*'), interspersed with appropriately poignant quotes from Homer's *Iliad*. Eighteen months of civil war followed. The year 69 is often now given the euphemistic title 'Year of the Four Emperors', as four aristocrats, each with the support of one of the regional armies (Spain, Danube, Rhine and Syria) competed for succession to the throne – wrecking the centre of Rome in the process and burning down the great temple of Jupiter on the Capitoline Hill. But the end result was the victory of a coalition backing Titus Flavius Vespasianus, now usually known simply as 'Vespasian'.

Vespasian was the general in charge of the Roman army suppressing the Jewish rebellion which had erupted in 66.

After a long siege and huge loss of life, Jerusalem was captured and ransacked under the immediate command of Vespasian's son, Titus, in 70. Scurrilous Jewish stories, preserved in the Talmud, told how Titus had desecrated the Holy of Holies by having sex with a prostitute on the holy scriptures (a sacrilege avenged by the good God who sent a flea which penetrated Titus' brain, drummed mercilessly inside his skull and – as was revealed by autopsy – caused a tumour which eventually killed him). Some Roman stories were hardly less fantastic. It was said that while still in the East Vespasian, as newly declared emperor, legitimated his rule by a series of miracles (curing the lame with his foot and the blind with the spittle from his lips). In fact, more prosaically, the emperor and prince spent a leisurely time in the rich eastern provinces raising taxes to repair the damage to state finances caused by Nero's extravagances. They returned to Rome – first Vespasian, then Titus – to celebrate a joint triumph over the Jews in 71.

This triumphal procession proclaimed the end of civil war, the supreme power of the Roman state and popular hopes for future happiness; or so we are told by a writer who may well have witnessed the ceremony, the historian Josephus, once himself a rebel Jewish commander, now a turncoat favourite at the Roman court. The two generals, dressed in ceremonial purple costume, travelling in a chariot drawn by white horses, made their way through the streets of Rome. In the procession, the conquering soldiers displayed a selection of their prisoners (apparently Titus had specially chosen the handsome ones) and their booty to cheering crowds: a mass of silver, gold, ivory and precious gems. Large wagons, like floats in a modern carnival, were decorated with

huge pictures of the war: a once prosperous countryside dev-
astated, rebels slaughtered, towns destroyed or on fire, prisoners praying for mercy. And from the Temple of Jerusalem
itself there came curtains ripped from the sanctuary (and
destined to decorate Vespasian's palace), a scroll containing
the Jewish Law, a solid-gold table and the seven-branched
candelabra, the Menorah, whose image still clearly stands
out on the triumphal arch in honour of Titus at the east end
of the Forum (illustration 6). On the ruined Capitoline hill,
the procession halted in front of the Temple of Jupiter Best
and Greatest. Only after Simon son of Gioras, the defeated
Jewish general, had been executed did Vespasian and Titus
say prayers and sacrifice; the people cheered and feasted at
public expense. Rome's imperial regime was safely restored.

The new emperor Vespasian's first task was to reconstruct
the ceremonial centre of Rome, to stamp his own identity on
the city and to wipe away the memory of Nero. He rebuilt
the Temple of Jupiter and constructed a vast new Temple
of 'Peace', a celebration of Rome's military success
('Pacification' might be a better title) as much as its civilising
mission. The obvious problem, however, was what to do with
the most notorious of Nero's building schemes: his vast
palace known as the Golden House, whose parkland had
taken over a substantial swathe of the city centre, up to 120
hectares (300 acres) in some modern (and probably exaggerated) estimates. The surviving wing of this architectural
extravaganza amounts to some 150 rooms preserved in the
foundation of the later Baths of Trajan and now after years of
closure partly accessible to the public once more (though the
famous painted decoration is sadly dilapidated and nothing
to compare with what Raphael and his friends saw when they

6. A sculptured panel on Arch of Titus in Rome depicts the parade of booty from the sack of Jerusalem in the triumphal procession of AD 71. As this seventeenth-century engraving shows more clearly than the now eroded original sculpture, the menorah from the Temple was given pride of place among the spoils.

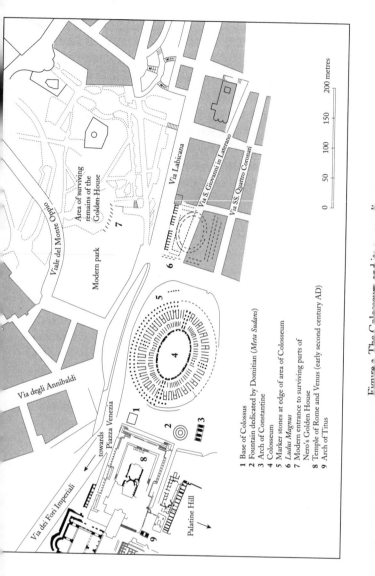

1 Base of Colossus
2 Fountain dedicated by Domitian (*Meta Sudans*)
3 Arch of Constantine
4 Colosseum
5 Marker stones at edge of area of Colosseum
6 *Ludus Magnus*
7 Modern entrance to surviving parts of Nero's Golden House
8 Temple of Rome and Venus (early second century AD)
9 Arch of Titus

Figure 2 The Colosseum and its surroundings

rediscovered the site in the sixteenth century). Originally the Golden House's highlights were said to have included a state-of-the-art dining room with revolving ceiling, a colossal bronze statue, more than likely representing Nero himself, some 30 metres tall, and a private lake – 'more like a sea than a lake', according to Nero's Roman biographer, Suetonius – surrounded by buildings made to represent cities. Much of the ancient report of this palace is overblown. Recent excavation on the site of the lake, for example, has suggested that far from being 'more like a sea', with all the images of wild nature that implies, it was a relatively small, rather formal affair. And there is no good reason to suppose, as was alleged soon after, that Nero had himself started the great fire of Rome in 64, simply in order to get his hands on vacant building land (even if he took advantage of the trail of emptiness and devastation the fire had left in bringing his grandiose schemes to fruition). Nonetheless there seems to have been a strong view at the time that the Golden House was monopolising, for the emperor's private pleasure, space in the centre of the city that by rights belonged to the Roman people. 'Citizens emigrate to Veii, Rome has become a single house', as one squib put it at the time.

Vespasian's response was shrewd and practical. Part of the Golden House appears to have continued in imperial use (and there is a good case for suggesting that Titus had his residence there a good decade after Nero's death). But on the site of that infamous private lake he founded what we now call the Colosseum, a pleasure palace for the people. It was a brilliantly calculated political gesture to obliterate Nero's memory with a monument to public entertainment, and by giving back to popular use space that had been monopolised by private imperial luxury. And it was a theme harped on by Martial in the second poem of his celebratory volume, which marked the opening of the building almost ten years later, under Titus, in 80 (Vespasian himself did not live to see its final completion, dying in 79). To quote Killigrew's translation again, which hails the emperor, as Martial's original did, under the Latin title 'Caesar':

> Where the stupendious theatre's vast Pile
> Is rear'd, there *Nero*'s Fish-ponds were e'er while
>
> …
>
> *Rome*'s to it self restor'd; in *Caesar*'s Reign
> The Prince's Pleasures now the People gain.

But it was more than just a question of the return of the city's space to popular use. In building the Colosseum Vespasian was dramatically making the point that the profits of Roman military success belonged, in part at least, to the common people of Rome; it was not only emperor and aristocracy who were to enrich themselves with the booty of empire. For, where did the money come from to build this vast monument? Some of it, almost certainly, from the mass of precious spoils that flowed into Rome with the suppression of the Jewish rebellion. In fact, it may even be that monumental inscriptions in the Colosseum emphasised exactly this point. Or so an ingenious recent discovery has been taken to suggest.

A few years ago archaeologists minutely re-examined a large inscribed block of stone that had been known for centuries; it once was lying around in the arena and made a convenient resting place for the weary Victorian tourist. The main text on this block was carved in the fifth century and commemorates a restoration of the Colosseum in that period. But it was noticed that the block had had an earlier use and had once carried a quite different text displayed in bronze letters – to judge from the dowel-holes which had fixed these letters and were still visible. Careful tracing and measurement of the holes allowed the original wording to be reconstructed. The Latin (illustration 7) means:

THE EMPEROR VESPASIAN ORDERED THIS NEW AMPHITHEATRE
TO BE CONSTRUCTED FROM THE BOOTY ...

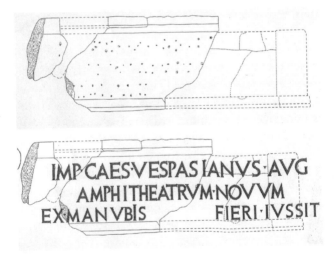

7. Joining the dots? The dowel holes (above) reconstructed into the dedicatory inscription of the Colosseum (below).

Whether this reconstruction is the result of a brilliant piece of academic detective work or the combination of vivid imagination and wishful thinking depends on your point of view. A sceptical reader is likely to feel (as we do) that there is an uncomfortably long distance between the scatter of holes and the suspiciously appropriate solution to 'joining the dots'. Nonetheless, inscribed text or no inscribed text, the underlying point remains. The Roman Colosseum was the fruit of Roman victory over the Jews. It was, in effect, the Temple of Jerusalem transformed by Roman culture, rebuilt for popular pleasure and the ostentatious display of imperial power.

There is, however, a sting in the tail of this story of the amphitheatre's construction and its original message. For if part of Vespasian's intention was to dislodge Nero from Rome's 'sites of memory', he notably failed. For by the Middle Ages the building had taken on the name by which we now know it: Colosseum. This was not simply because it was very big; though sheer size must have been one factor in explaining why what was originally a nickname has so firmly stuck. The most likely derivation is from the colossal statue of Nero (the 'Colossus') that stood near by, commissioned by him for his Golden House. There have been all kinds of modern disputes about this statue. Was it actually completed before Nero's death? Was it meant to stand in the vestibule of the Golden House, as many people (but not all) have taken Suetonius' biography of Nero to suggest? Did it represent Nero or the Sun God, or Nero *as* the Sun God? And how, anyway, would you tell the difference? Whatever the answer to these questions, it is clear enough that it long outlasted Nero's palace itself, albeit with a series of alterations to its facial features (down-playing the Neronian characteristics) to bring it more acceptably into line with the changing imperial regimes, and with a wholesale shift of site under the emperor Hadrian – with the help of an architect and twenty-four elephants. There is evidence that it was still standing in the fourth century, on a base near the Colosseum which was destroyed only in the 1930s, when Mussolini had the area 'cleaned up' to make way for his new road, the modern Via dei Fori Imperiali. And it may well be that the famous slogan quoted in a collection (wrongly) attributed to the eighth-century scholar Bede, 'So long as the *Colisaeus* stands, Rome also stands, when the *Colisaeus* falls, Rome will fall too', refers to the statue and not, as it is usually taken (partly because it makes a better prediction), to the amphitheatre.

The irony is, then, that the standard modern name for Vespasian's great amphitheatre is one that makes it more of a memorial to Nero than to the dynasty that replaced him. So much so that popular imagination often sees it as a Neronian monument and films (from Cecil B. DeMille's *Sign of the Cross* to Mervyn Le Roy's *Quo Vadis*) have blithely envisaged Nero presiding over the massacre of Christians there – almost two decades before it would in fact have been built. For us the Colosseum must offer more than a political message about the Roman people's stake in the city and its empire. It embodies an important lesson in the ambiguities of memory, obliteration and amnesia. Wiping an emperor out of the landscape was more difficult than it may seem; as always, the harder you try, the more you risk drawing the attention of history to what you are trying to remove. Even without its Neronian-medieval name, Vespasian's amphitheatre was always likely to be remembered as the monument which stood on the site of Nero's lake.

The symbolic power of the Colosseum in ancient Rome depended also on political issues that went far beyond the immediate circumstances of its construction. It came to be seen as one of the most important arenas (in the metaphorical as well as the literal sense) in which the emperor came face to face with his people – and to stand as a symbol of the encounter between autocrat and those he ruled. To understand how and why this was so, we need to consider briefly the wider context of the history of Roman politics – and the history of amphitheatres.

For us, the Colosseum is such a well-known part of the Roman skyline that it is easy to forget that, in the AD 70s, the construction of a huge stone amphitheatre in the centre of the city constituted a break with tradition. To be sure, other Italian and provincial cities in the Roman empire had long had amphitheatres of their own: for example, Pompeii (the earliest surviving amphitheatre from about 70 BC), Verona and Milan in Italy, Lyon in France, Merida in Spain and Carthage in Tunisia. And many more were to come as far afield as Jerusalem and London (where remains of the structure roughly contemporary with the Colosseum were discovered under the Guildhall in 1988). In Rome, however, before the Colosseum was built, people had generally watched gladiatorial shows in temporary structures. True, a Roman aristocrat in the reign of the emperor Augustus (31 BC to AD 14) had built a smallish amphitheatre at least partly in stone. But this was hardly grand enough for big shows (certainly the emperor Caligula is reported to have looked down his nose at it) and, in any case, like so much else in the capital, it had been burnt down in the great fire of 64. Standard practice was to build a wooden amphitheatre and take it down when the shows were over, or to make use of public buildings designed with other purposes in mind. Massive shows were occasionally given in the Circus Maximus, where chariot races were held, or in the so-called Voting Pens (or 'Saepta', the vast structure designed to accommodate mass voting by Roman citizens); but both venues were too large for normal displays. More often the gladiators performed in the Forum itself, the audience watching from wooden benches, which would have been dismantled at the end of the day.

Some of these temporary structures, and their fittings, were impressive enough in their own right. Pliny, the insufferable polymath and moraliser who was killed in the eruption of Vesuvius in AD 79, claims that the vast awning which Julius Caesar on one occasion used to cover the whole of the Forum, from one end to the other, was thought more 'amazing' than the gladiatorial show itself. And he tells in gleeful horror of a 'mad fantasy in wood' constructed by one of Cicero's friends in the first century BC. This consisted in two adjacent semicircular wooden theatres, mounted on revolving pivots, which could be swivelled together to make a completely enclosed *amphi*theatre. Apparently, rather like coupling a train with the passengers on board, the whole operation of joining the two halves could be carried out with the spectators in their seats. Pliny was appalled: 'Just imagine the people who have conquered the earth and have subdued the whole world, who govern tribes and kingdoms, who give their laws to the outside world, who are, you might say, a part of heaven on earth – just imagine them balanced on the contraption and applauding their own danger!' Many more Romans, we suspect, would have been impressed at the

[37]

splendid ingenuity of the device. Certainly, a poet in the reign of Nero imagines two rustics visiting the city overwhelmed by the sight of the emperor's new wooden amphitheatre (even without the mechanical sophistication). They stand 'rooted to the spot, mouth agape' and (in terms reminiscent of Constantius' reported reactions to the Colosseum) they reckon that it is almost as high as the Capitoline hill itself.

Of course, it was not – even if, as Pliny claimed, the largest tree ever seen at Rome, a vast larch that produced a log 40 metres long, was used in its construction. However extravagantly these earlier structures might be written up, in the late first century the Colosseum was something new for the city of Rome itself, in scale and permanence. Why did the innovation of a permanent amphitheatre take so long?

Traditionally, the Roman elite had always been chary of building in Rome a permanent monument to pleasure. It smacked too much of the luxury and decadence that Romans were anxious simultaneously to embrace and to avoid. More importantly yet, in the period of the Republic (conventionally dated from around 500 to 31 BC), when Rome was governed by elected officials or 'magistrates' and by a Senate made up largely of ex-magistrates – all of them wealthy aristocrats – senators may have been realistically afraid of providing a venue where the mass of citizens could express their views collectively and vociferously. It did not matter much to the Senate what citizens in Pompeii or Bologna thought or did (though a riot in the amphitheatre at Pompeii under the emperor Nero in AD 59 was severely punished by a ten-year ban on gladiator shows). But in Rome itself under the Republic, citizens had a much more direct influence over the passage of laws and the election of senators to further offices. At the same time, citizen voters were also then, potentially at least, soldiers. Their power to vote was a reflection of their power to fight, and vice versa. Mass gatherings, even if apparently for pleasure, must have seemed a dangerous commodity in the eyes of the elite.

That changed in significant ways with the advent of the Roman emperors. By the mid first century BC the Republican system of government had imploded. Out of a series of civil wars, juntas and dictatorships (culminating in the one-man rule and assassination in 44 BC of Julius Caesar), a more-or-less hereditary monarchy emerged, under the first emperor or 'princeps', Augustus. Under the emperors, the bulk of the army was dispersed along distant frontiers and soldiers were recruited predominantly from provincials. The citizens of Italy, with the vital exception of the Palace Guard, were effectively disarmed. And so it became practicable for the emperors to disenfranchise citizens living in Rome. Soon (even if not immediately with the advent of monarchy) elections were transferred from people to Senate. The once warlike 'masters of the [Western] world', as the Roman poet Virgil called them, were – to give it the most cynical spin – gratefully bribed with monthly distributions of free wheat and with frequent shows. This disenfranchisement of the Roman people was probably not part of a magnificently conceived master plan. But, however it evolved, it significantly increased monarchical power. The process is nicely symbolised by the history of the Voting Pens. The emperor Augustus, in honour of Rome's long tradition of popular participation in politics, had erected these to upgrade the old Republican voting enclosure. They were the largest covered building in Rome. If initially citizen voting continued, however, by the end of the first century AD these Pens were no longer used for voting. Instead they had become a venue for large shows, as we have seen, and a giant supermarket for antiques. Democracy, in the traditional sense, was almost dead.

By the time the Colosseum was inaugurated in AD 80, monarchy was so firmly entrenched that emperors could readily risk, even periodically enjoy, confronting their citizen-subjects collectively. More than that, it was essential to their power-base that they should see, and – even more crucially – be seen by, the people at large. Whatever the harsher realities, there was always the ideal or myth that citizens had the right of access to the emperor, to ask a favour, to correct an injustice, to hand in a petition. One illusion on which the Roman monarchy was founded was that the emperor was only the first aristocrat among equals, and one of the emperor's titles right from the beginning cast him in the role of Tribune (or Protector) of the People. No other ancient monarchy, whether in Persia, Egypt, India or China, ever staged such regular meetings between ruler and subjects. In fact, an ancient Chinese visitor to the Roman empire thought the public accessibility of the emperor quite extraordinary: 'When the king goes out he usually gets one of his suite to follow him with a leather bag, into which petitioners throw a statement of their case; on arrival at the palace, the king examines the merits of each case.'

Of course, the Roman people had their fond illusions too: they thought that they could, occasionally at least, collectively influence what the emperor did by letting their rhythmically chanted views be heard.

There were other locations, to be sure, where the emperor could confront his people: in the Forum, for example, or in the Circus Maximus. But the Forum was small by comparison, and the Circus was if anything too huge to concentrate the popular voice. The Colosseum was a brilliantly constructed and enclosed world, which packed emperor, elite and subjects together, like sardines in a tin. Its steeply serried ranks of spectator-participants, watching and being watched, hierarchically ordered by status (by rule, the higher ranks sat near the front, the masses at the back), faced each other across the arena in the round. It was a magnificent setting for a ruler to parade his power before his citizen-subjects; and for those subjects to show – or at least fantasise about showing – their collective muscle in front of the emperor.

The Colosseum was very much more than a sports venue. It was a political theatre in which each stratum of Roman society played out its role (ideally at least; there were times, as we shall see in Chapter 4, that this – like all political theatre – went horribly and subversively wrong). The emperor knew he was emperor best when cheered by the ovations of an enthusiastic crowd who were seduced by the prospect of violent death (whether of animals or humans), by the gifts the emperor would occasionally have showered amongst the spectators and by the sheer excitement of being there. The Roman elite in the front seats would have paraded their status, nodding to their friends: this surely was where business contracts, promotion, alliances, marriages were first mentioned or followed up. The crowd, usually grateful and compliant, sometimes chanted for the end of a war or for more shows – seeing their power *as the Roman people* all round the arena. It was a vital part of Roman political life to be there, to be seen to be there and to watch the others. Hence the building's iconic status for the Romans, as well as for us.

3

THE KILLING FIELDS

AD 80: OPENING EVENTS

The Colosseum was officially opened under the new emperor Titus in AD 80, in an extravaganza of fighting, beast hunts and bloodshed that is said to have lasted a hundred days. The scale of the slaughter is hard to estimate. We have no figures at all for deaths among the gladiators, but Titus' biographer, Suetonius, claims that during these celebrations (though not necessarily in the Colosseum itself) 'on a single day' 5000 animals were killed – a claim that has been boldly re-interpreted by a few modern scholars to mean 'on *every* single day' of the performance, so giving a vast, and frankly implausible, total of half a million animal casualties. One of the fullest accounts of the proceedings, by the historian Dio writing in the third century, is rather more modest in its estimates: he reckons that 9000 animals were slain in all. But elsewhere, discussing games given by Julius Caesar in 46 BC, Dio reflects on the difficulty of calculating the correct tally of fighters or victims. 'If anyone wanted to record their number,' he complains, 'they would have trouble finding out and it would not necessarily be an accurate account. For all things of this sort get exaggerated and hyped.' The Roman audience's appetite for slaughter was presumably well matched by the capacity for boasting on the part of those who put on the shows.

Many of the practical arrangements are also tricky to reconstruct. One question that has puzzled archaeologists and historians for centuries is whether or not the central arena was flooded during these opening games. Dio writes confidently of how 'Titus suddenly filled the arena with water and brought in horses and bulls and other domesticated animals which had been taught to swim' (if 'swimming' is what Dio means when he says, literally, 'had been taught to behave in liquid just as they did on dry land'). And he goes on to describe Titus producing ships and staging a mock sea-battle, apparently recreating one of the famous naval encounters of fifth-century BC Greece, between the forces of the cities of Corcyra and Corinth. This extraordinary spectacle would certainly not be possible in the building as it survives today, for there is no way that the basement of the arena (with its intricate set of lifts and other contraptions for hoisting animals) could be waterproofed. Maybe when the amphitheatre was first built, before the insertion of all that clever machinery, it had ingeniously allowed for the option of flooding. Or maybe Dio was mistaken. Suetonius, in his account, certainly suggests that the water displays took place in a quite different purpose-built location. Even Dio himself, in describing the spectacles that must have spread widely over the city during the hundred days, has some of the water sports – including another mock naval battle, this time apparently involving 3000 men – staged in a special facility constructed by the first emperor Augustus.

Whether or not the Colosseum was miraculously converted back into a lake (which would have been a neat joke on Nero's private lake that the public amphitheatre had replaced), the range of displays put on for the building's inauguration were the most lavish that Roman money and imperial power could buy. Dio again refers tantalisingly to fights staged between elephants and between cranes – though exactly how they made these birds fight each other is hard (or awful) to imagine. He also mentions that women were involved in the wild beast hunts, while being at pains to reassure us that these were not women 'of social distinction'. But the most vivid recreations of these spectacular events are found in Martial's book of poems (*The Book of the Shows*) which was written to commemorate the opening of the amphitheatre. Exaggerated flattery of his imperial patron Titus, these verses may have been. There is no doubt a good deal of wishful thinking and poetic licence in the details of the spectacles described. Nonetheless, this book is one of the very rare cases where we can bring together a work of ancient literature, a specific ancient building and what happened in it on one particular occasion. The poems help us to glimpse not only what might have taken place there, but what a sophisti- cated Roman audience might have found to admire in these horrible, bloodthirsty performances. They bring us face to face with the (in Roman terms) exquisite inventiveness of cruelty.

Martial starts by praising the building ('All Works to *Caesar's* Theatre give place') and then stops briefly to high- light the exotic, polyglot crowd which has turned up for the greatest show on earth: a wonderful combination of farmers from the wilds of northern Greece, the weird Sarmatians from the Danube who drink their horses' blood, and Germans and Ethiopians, each sporting a different style of curly hair. The first 'act' he celebrates is one that modern readers must find most shocking. It is not from what we now imagine to be the standard repertoire of these shows: gladiators and wild beast hunts (or alternatively the execution of criminals by animals, as in 'Christians versus lions'). Instead, it is a strange 'charade', re-enacting a story from mythology – for the Romans a no less important and distinctive genre of displays in the amphitheatre. In this case the story played out is that of Pasiphae, the wife of King Minos of Crete whom the god Poseidon (in order to punish her husband) made fall in love with a bull: the famous half-bull/half-human Minotaur was the result of the union. Martial's poem appears to claim that this event was acted out before the audience in the amphitheatre, between a woman and a live animal, while praising the capacity of the show to 'make real' such ancient (even to the Romans) mythological tales. As Thomas May's, rather too gleeful, seventeenth-century translation puts it:

> Beleeve a bull enioy'd the Cretan Queene;
> Th'old fable verif'd we all have seene.
> Let not old times, Caesar, selfe-praised bee;
> Since what fame sings, the stage presents to thee.

How literally should we read this? Are we to take it that these opening celebrations of the Colosseum, under the admiring eye of the emperor Titus and of the massed ranks of Roman citizens, really featured sex between a woman and a bull? Possibly. There is other evidence for dramatic executions of criminals in the Roman arena along these lines (presumably the woman would not have survived the encounter, which we assume to have been some form of quasi-judicial punishment). Condemned criminals were induced – again, it is difficult to see quite how – to take part in their own death scenes as if actors in a play. Later in *The Book of the Shows* Martial focuses on the crucifixion of a man, who seems to have re-enacted in the amphitheatre the punishment of a legendary Roman bandit called Laureolus, until he was put out of his misery by a bear imported from Scotland. He simultaneously reminded the audience of the myth of Prometheus, whose particular divine punishment was to have his liver continually devoured by vultures during the day and grow back again at night:

> Just as Prometheus, bound tight on a Russian crag
> Fed with his ever healing and regrowing heart
> The bird that never tires of eating
> So,
> cast as
> Laureolus, the bandit king, nailed to a cross – no stage
> prop this –
> A man offered his exposed guts to a Highland bear.
> His shredded limbs clung onto life though
> Their constituent parts gushed with blood;
> No trace of body – but the body lived.
> Finally he got the punishment he deserved …
> Maybe he'd slit his master's throat,
> Maybe he'd robbed a temple's treasury of gold,
> Maybe he'd tried to burn our city, Rome.
> That criminal had surpassed all ancient folklore's crimes.
> Through him what had been merely myth
> Became real punishment.

This is also an aspect of games, that Tertullian – a late second-century Christian from North Africa, and a particularly strident religious ideologue – picks out when he complains that criminals in the amphitheatre take on the mythological roles of Attis (who castrated himself) or Hercules (burned alive). Even closer to Martial's woman and the bull is an episode in Apuleius' brilliant novel *The Golden Ass*, also a product of second-century North Africa. Apuleius recounts how a woman convicted of murder was condemned, before being eaten by a beast, to have intercourse in a local amphitheatre with an ass – in fact the human hero of the story, transformed into an ass by a magical accident. The brainy ass is not convinced that the lion will know the script, and fears that it might well eat him instead of the woman, so he scarpers before the performance.

On the other hand, we might be dealing with a rather different kind of charade. It is not so much a question of how feasible the intercourse described would be; historians have been predictably ingenious with their solutions to that problem, and have plenty of parallels from modern pornography to hand. More to the point is that there is nothing here to disprove the idea that the 'bull' was in fact a human being in fancy dress and that the 'reality' of the union was something injected by the poet. After all, the wonderfully fantastical *Golden Ass* and the tirades of Tertullian are hardly very strong evidence for standard practice in the arena. Martial's contribution to the celebration, in other words, might have been to take a piece of play-acting in the Colosseum and to *make it real* (by treating it as such) in his verses.

Whatever reconstruction they prefer, most modern scholars have been keen to stress that Martial did not disapprove of such spectacles. True enough. But by using approval or disapproval as the touchstone, this observation tends to miss what Martial so positively admires in the shows and spectacles that he evokes and recreates for his readers. In contrast to the common modern view of the crude sadism of the arena, Martial's poems repeatedly emphasise – uncomfortable as this must be for us – the sophistication of what was on show at the Colosseum's inauguration, its clever echoes of the cultural and mythological inheritance of the Roman world, and the wily thoughts about representation and reality ('what had been merely myth became real punishment') they prompt. Perhaps the most puzzling thing about the Roman amphitheatre is not how to explain the violence and cruelty that took place there, but how to explain the way the Romans described and explained that violence.

In the other thirty or so poems that make up the celebratory collection for the Colosseum's opening, Martial develops these themes. One playfully (and horribly) subverts the myth of Orpheus, the magician who could charm the animals: the Orpheus figure in this display works no such magic – he is torn apart by a bear. No fewer than three poems take as their subject a pregnant sow killed in one of the beast hunts: in a striking coincidence of birth and death, baby piglets emerged from the very wound made by the spear. Others reflect on the miraculous shifts engineered between water and dry land (so perhaps supporting Dio's claims about the flooding) and on the paradoxes of the wild and the tame that were on show in the amphitheatre. A tigress, for example, scored a first by attacking a lion when she would have done no such thing in the wild: the truth was that domestication had actually increased her ferocity.

Conversely, an elephant that had just dispatched a bull spontaneously came and knelt as a suppliant in front of the emperor; so too did a deer, who in this way miraculously escaped the hounds chasing her. The message – all the stronger for being delivered in this mass gathering – was that even the animals recognised imperial power.

But what of the gladiators? Only one single poem in the whole *Book of the Shows* features a gladiatorial bout. We must assume that the hundred days of celebration saw combat after combat between the usual array of star fighters, hardened veterans and raw recruits. But here one encounter must stand for all. The fighters concerned were 'Priscus' and 'Verus', both (stage-)names with a ring: 'Ancient' and 'True'. They were such an evenly matched pair that the crowd demanded their honourable discharge from gladiatorial service (their 'mission', as Killigrew's translation has it) and in the end the fight had to be declared a draw. But, as so often, the eye of the poet (if not of the audience on the day; who knows?) was as much on the emperor as on the spectacle in the arena itself. It is Titus, we are told, who enforced the terms for the bout, Titus who sent them rich rewards for their valour, apparently while the fight was still in progress, and finally Titus who sent them the palms to mark their (joint) victory.

> *Priscus* and *Verus*, while with equal Might,
> Prolong'd an obstinate and doubtful Fight,
> The People, oft, their mission did desire;
> But *Caesar* from the law would not retire,
> Which did the Prize and Victory unite,
> Yet gave them what Encouragement he might;

> Largess of Meat and Money did bestow,
> Which also 'mong the People he did throw,
> I' the'end, howe'er, the Strife was equal found,
> Both fought alike, and both alike gave ground:
> So that the Palm was upon each conferr'd,
> Their undecided Valour this deserv'd.
> Under no Prince before we e'er did see
> That two should fight, and both should Victors be.

Given our own image of these bloody combats, it is perhaps surprising that this courageous but apparently bloodless draw should be the only gladiatorial fight commemorated at the inaugural games in the Colosseum. Even more surprising is that – so far as we have been able to discover, at least – this poem is the only account of a specific gladiatorial bout to survive from the ancient world. We have plenty of boastful claims of gladiatorial numbers, a good deal of discussion about the appeal of the gladiators themselves and the valour, or the horror, of the fighting, not to mention tombstones recording their death in the arena, and countless images of these distinctively dressed combatants, decorating everything from cheap oil lamps to costly mosaic floors. Yet the only thing approaching a description of an actual contest between two individual gladiators is this tale of imperial generosity and the ancient equivalent of a goalless draw in AD 80.

ON WITH THE SHOW

Spectacular shows over many days, such as those that opened the Colosseum, were infrequent – though much trumpeted – events in the monument's history. The enthusiasm of individual emperors for these spectacles varied considerably, as did their generosity. Some were notoriously stingy. Others gave special games to celebrate the anniversary of their succession, for their birthday or victory over foreign enemies, or even to commemorate the glories of a predecessor. In the first decade of the second century, for example, the emperor Trajan gave the biggest bloodbath ever recorded, presumably in the Colosseum, to celebrate his conquest of Dacia (modern Romania). Dio again has some facts and figures: the shows took place on 123 days; 11,000 animals were killed, 10,000 gladiators fought. This time we have more details not from poetry written to commemorate the occasion, but from a record included in a calendar of public events inscribed in stone, from Rome's port of Ostia. This more or less matches Dio's picture of the scale of the events, but also makes clear that the celebrations did not take place in one continuous 'sitting' of more than a hundred days of solid slaughter. Instead they were broken down into smaller units. First, in 107 and 108, there were preliminary games in blocks of twelve or thirteen days, with over 300 pairs of gladiators at each. Then came the main show, which according to the inscription was staged on 117 days between June 108 and November 109 and involved '4941 and a half pairs of gladiators' (the 'half pair' being a good indication that gladiators who survived one bout might fight again later in the same show – otherwise whom did the stray 'half' fight?). Maybe Titus' inaugural games were divided up in this way too. It would certainly have made the organisation of animals and human fighters easier, and no doubt also have ensured a keener crowd. The idea that the Romans happily devoted weeks and weeks on end to watching displays of unadulterated slaughter in the

Colosseum is probably a modern fantasy. Titus and Trajan would have understood the value of breaking the monotony, and of rationing the violence.

The regular performances in the Colosseum were not these blockbuster shows sponsored by emperors. It had been a tradition going back decades before the building of the Colosseum that Roman aristocrats would present shows – involving gladiatorial combat or wild beast hunts and displays, or a combination of the two – as part of their bid for popularity with the Roman people. These were the occasions that took place in the Forum or in temporary amphitheatres. Whatever the dangers of mass gatherings of the electorate, in the toughly competitive politics of the city of Rome, particularly in the years just before the advent of monarchy under Augustus, a good performance no doubt enormously helped a man's chances of winning prestige and public office. Shows hosted by aristocrats outside the imperial family certainly continued through the first century AD and presumably after 80 also took place in the Colosseum. We say 'presumably' because ancient writers were so fixated on the emperor's shows that they give us precious few details of any others.

Many of these may have been by the emperor's standards modest, even amateurish, occasions, with a restricted repertoire of both gladiators and beasts, a long way from the popular image of sadistic excess. In fact, legislation was enacted and re-enacted through the Roman empire to limit the number of gladiators an 'ordinary' aristocrat might present and to regulate the displays. It was, after all, in the emperor's interest to prevent potential rivals currying popular favour with lavish spectacles. But some aristocrats did evade the restrictions (which may not have been consistently or efficiently enforced anyway) and poured money into shows to enhance their public image. Even when it was centuries since they had been obliged to seek the votes of the people, their reputations still depended on ostentatious success. And, instead of a dangerous rivalry, some emperors may have felt that it was a relatively harmless way for them to spend their money.

At the end of the fourth century, a man by the name of Symmachus (a well-known defender of traditional Roman religion against the growth of Christianity), more than once invested huge amounts of time and wealth in funding shows to mark the public advancement of his son. We read in his *Letters* of his attempts to acquire exotic beasts: antelopes, bears, leopards and lions. It was not always worth the trouble or the cash. The bear cubs that he procured, for example, turned out to be emaciated specimens, but at least not quite the disaster that the Saxon gladiators were: twenty-nine of these strangled each other on the evening before their scheduled performance. But disasters or not, it was all phenomenally expensive. One Roman historian, whose work now survives only in snippets quoted by later writers, reckoned that Symmachus spent 2000 pounds of gold (in standard ancient Roman currency 9 million sesterces) to celebrate his son's tenure of the office of praetor. That is a sum large enough to feed nearly 20,000 peasant families for a year at minimum subsistence, or nine times the minimum fortune required to qualify for senatorial rank, the topmost elite of Roman society. Allow for some exaggeration and suppose only 20 per cent of it went on the show; it still gives an idea of the level of expenditure that might be involved.

In the end it is hard for us to know how to visualise the

Colosseum in Roman times. One picture is very much that offered by epic movies: an auditorium packed with spectators, an arena covered with animals, beast hunters and gladiators, and dripping with blood. The other is a much more everyday, low-key image: an auditorium hardly bursting at the seams, with a rather tame troupe of B-team gladiators and some mangy animals that have seen better days. That is always the dilemma with imagining Rome. Do we embrace the larger-than-life vision that is projected by later writers and by many Roman writers themselves? Or do we cynically suspect that for most of the time, outside a few very special occasions, the reality was a lot less impressive, frankly rather tawdry? And how do we decide?

The same dilemma confronts us when we come to ask how often the Colosseum was in use. For Trajan's celebrations of his Dacian victory through 108–9, it was apparently hosting performances almost one day out of five. But what was 'normal'? No one knows. Strikingly few days, though, are assigned to 'regular' gladiatorial games in any of the Roman calendars that have been preserved: in the fourth century AD it seems that, out of 176 days of 'holiday', just over a hundred were devoted to theatrical shows, sixty-four to horse and chariot racing and only ten days to gladiatorial games. Are we to imagine that, outside special occasions, the Colosseum would have been mothballed? Or that it would have been a constant bustle of workmen and administrators clearing up the mess, getting ready for the next show and doing running repairs on the fabric and machinery? Or that, for much of the year, it provided a convenient home for all kinds of other activities that readily colonised its city-centre location, a place to flog your wares, take a nap, sight-see or make a pick-up? Again, no one knows. But when we reflect on the significance of the shows that took place in the Colosseum, it is worth remembering that, as with Christmas, sheer frequency is not necessarily a good guide to cultural importance.

'HAIL CAESAR. THOSE ABOUT TO DIE SALUTE YOU'?

To read most modern accounts of the shows in the Colosseum (or indeed of those, admittedly smaller-scale, displays in amphitheatres all over the Roman empire) you would think that a handbook to such events survived from the ancient world – or at the very least a series of programmes, laying out in detail the order of ceremonies according to a standard pattern. We are repeatedly told that the sequence of the day's events in the arena was fixed by rule or custom. In the morning were the wild animal hunts: more or less exotic species (and the more exotic the better, of course) put to fight each other or pitted against trained marksmen and hunters, some on horseback, others on foot, picking the animals off with spear, sword or arrow. In the 'lunch break' came the public executions, either in the 'mythological' form that Martial evokes, or in other varieties of ingenious slaughter and torture (including the notorious lions), or just plain killing.

It was not until the afternoon, so it was said, that the gladiatorial bouts proper began. The fighters entered, hailed the emperor with the famous words 'Those about to die salute you' and the real fun started. They sported different types of armour and weaponry, and had adopted a range of fighting styles: there were 'net-men', for example, heavy-armed 'Thracians' and 'Samnites', and *murmillones* or 'fish-heads' (so

[55]

called after the emblem on their helmets). Although all kinds of formation were possible, they usually fought in pairs, one to one, trainers and umpires on hand to supervise the carnage, stretcher bearers (dressed as gods of the Underworld) to carry out the dead and wounded, as well as a blacksmith and forge for instant repairs. The victors may have been handsomely rewarded with popular fame, lavish presents from the sponsor of the show and ultimately (as was the fate of Priscus and Verus) with an honourable discharge. A wounded or defeated gladiator, on the other hand, was at the mercy of the audience. He would hold up his little finger as a sign of surrender, at which point the crowd would roar their preference for killing or sparing, putting their thumbs up or down. Many of the onlookers probably had a vested interest in the outcome and a small fortune staked on individual fighters (in fact the night before the show, the gladiators had their last meal *in public*, which gave aficionados a chance to study their form before placing their bets). But it was finally up to the sponsor to decide whether to spare the man's life or have him killed.

This is the scene captured in perhaps the most evocative modern painting of the Colosseum's arena (illustration 8). Jean-Léon Gérôme's canvas, painted in the early 1870s, shows a victorious combatant standing triumphant over a 'net-man' (or *retiarius*; his trademark net and trident have fallen to his right), who seems to have collapsed over a fighter dead or injured from a previous bout, but not yet cleared out of the arena. The victor wears one of those elaborate helmets distinctive of several types of gladiator, here decorated with a fish – though it is hard to pick out except on the original (now in Phoenix, Arizona) or on very large-scale reproductions. He is meant to be a *murmillo*. Equally distinctively, he

8. Jean-Léon Gérôme's painting, *Pollice Verso* ('Thumbs turned'), captures the
moment when the audience demand the slaughter of the defeated gladiator.
Its reconstruction not only of the gladiators' costumes, but also of the
decoration surrounding the arena, lies behind many later recreations of the
Colosseum, including Ridley Scott's in *Gladiator*.

displays a large amount of naked flesh. For one striking feature of Roman gladiatorial combat, compared with medieval jousting and knights all protected in their chain mail, was the exposure of so much of the bare body; it is as if they had to be visibly vulnerable. We are witnessing here those tense few moments while the winner waits for a sign from the emperor, seen sitting in his imperial box in the carefully reconstructed Colosseum. Kill or not? But our attention is drawn to the women on the front row (presumably the Vestal Virgins, the priestesses who were, as we shall see in Chapter 4, the only women allowed to watch from these ringside seats). With disconcerting eagerness they are signalling their desire for the kill, thumbs down. In fact, the title of the painting is the Latin phrase '*Pollice Verso*', literally 'Thumbs turned' – the phrase used by Roman writers to indicate the vote for a kill. Despite modern scholars' often confident claims to the contrary, we do not actually know in which direction Romans 'turned their thumbs'. It may have been 'up' for death and 'down' for mercy; or, as Gérôme imagines it, vice versa.

This is the painting that is supposed to have inspired the director of *Gladiator*, Ridley Scott: 'That image spoke to me of the Roman Empire in all its glory and wickedness,' he is quoted as saying. 'I knew right then and there I was hooked.' It also forms a sequel to another painting of Gérôme's, finished a decade or so earlier in 1859. In this other canvas (which has ended up in Yale University Art Gallery) we see a small posse of gladiators who have just entered the Colosseum's arena – obviously not the first fighters of the day, to judge from the corpse past which they have just had to walk. They raise their arms to acknowledge the emperor. The

9. Asterix and Obelix refuse to utter the famous greeting to Caesar before the gladiatorial games (and are inadvertently more historically accurate than the well-trained posse of fighters in front of them). Not so accurate is the setting. The Colosseum was not yet built at the time the plucky Gauls were outwitting Julius Caesar.

title of the painting, again in Latin, is that famous phrase: '*Ave Caesar. Morituri te salutant!*' 'Hail Caesar. Those about to die salute you!'

Sadly, there is no evidence at all that this phrase was ever uttered in the Colosseum, still less that it was the regular salute given by gladiators to the emperor. Ancient writers, in fact, quote it in relation to one specific spectacle only, and not a gladiatorial one. According to the biographer Suetonius – and Dio has much the same story – it was the phrase used by the 'naval fighters' ('*naumacharii*'; condemned criminals according to the historian Tacitus) in a spectacular mock battle on the Fucine Lake in the hills east of Rome, put on in AD 52 by the emperor Claudius, just before his almost equally spectacular feat of draining the lake. The story was that when the emperor heard the word '*morituri*' ('those who are about to die') he made a feeble joke by muttering 'or not, as the case may be'. Somehow the *naumacharii* picked this up and, taking it as a pardon, refused to fight. The emperor was forced to hobble off his throne and persuade the men back to the fight. This frankly implausible tale (how on earth were the fighters on the lake supposed to have heard the words muttered from the safe distance of the imperial throne?) is the only reference we have to the words which have become the slogan of gladiatorial combat in general, and of the Colosseum in particular, in modern culture (illustration 9).

Many of the other elements of the standard reconstruction of arena shows – whether in film, fiction, popular guidebooks or specialist accounts – are only slightly less tenuous. It is certainly the case, for example, that we have plenty of evidence for different types of gladiator, indicated by an array of carefully distinguished titles. Tombstones of fighters often specify this precisely. A wonderfully elaborate memorial from Rome commemorates a 'Thracian' from Alexandria, who came to Rome to take part in the shows in honour of the emperor Trajan's victories in AD 117; he did not live to go home (illustration 10). Another commemorates a gladiator who came from Florence, who died after thirteen fights at the age of twenty-two leaving a wife and two children (and blunt advice to anyone reading his tombstone 'to kill whoever you defeat'); he is said to have been a *secutor* ('Pursuer'). Meanwhile in poignant graffiti scratched on a wall at Herculaneum, a town that was to be buried under volcanic debris just as the building of the Colosseum in Rome was reaching completion, a gladiator vows his shield to the goddess Venus if he wins: his name is Mansuetus (a presumably ironic stage-name meaning 'Gentle'); he describes himself as a *provocator* ('Challenger'). It is clear enough too that these different types attracted their own groups of fans. The emperor Titus was, according to Suetonius, a self-confessed supporter of the Thracians and enjoyed arguing their merit with the crowd, just like any fan – 'though without losing his dignity or sense of justice', Suetonius assures us. Not so his younger brother Domitian, who was a follower of the *murmillones*. On one occasion, a man in the audience was heard to hint that it was impossible for a Thracian to win while the emperor was using his influence to secure a victory for the 'fish-heads'. In one of those mini dramas that must (in the telling, at least) have increased the excitement of the show, Domitian had him yanked out of the crowd and thrown to the dogs in the arena with an explanatory placard around his neck: *parmularius impie*. No translation can match the Latin's brevity: 'a Thracian fan, but sacrilegious'.

M. ANTONIVS EXOCHVS

T. H. R.
M. ANTONIVS
EXOCHVS NAT
ALEXANDRINVS
ROM. OB. TRIVMP.
DIVI TRAIANI DIE II
TIR CVM ARAXE CAE
ST. MISS.
ROM. MVN EIVS D.
DIE VIIII. FIMBRIAM
LIB VIIII. MISS FE
ROM. MVN. EIVS D.

Sub Quirinali.
I. Boissardi, Antiqq. Tix p. 132.

10. This illustration from an early collection of Roman inscriptions captures
a rather different image of a gladiator – much influenced, in this rendering,
by seventeenth-century style. The tombstone (now lost and no doubt
considerably restored in this picture) commemorates one Marcus Antonius
Exochus who, as the text explains, took part in gladiatorial games to
celebrate the triumph of the emperor Trajan in the early second century AD.

[62]

The trouble comes when we try to match up these different titles with the visual images of gladiators and gladiatorial fights in sculpture, graffiti, paintings and mosaics from places as far afield as Germany and Libya. For in the absence of any surviving ancient accounts which explain the typology, this is the only way that historians have hoped to work out the details of the different styles of costume and different fighting methods adopted by the various brands of combatant. Some distinct categories do emerge. There are clearly contrasting types of helmet. One, for example, seems entirely to cover the face apart from two tiny eye-holes. This is generally thought to belong to the *secutor* (title page). Others have a broad brim, and were probably worn by Thracians and *murmillones* (illustration 8, p. 57) – though the general absence of fish emblems makes some historians think that it was the overall 'fishy' shape that gave the *murmillo* his title. But most of the evidence resists easy categorisation. So, for example, despite their name, 'Net-men' are commonly shown with their tridents, but only very rarely shown carrying nets. Is this because ancient artists found nets a tricky subject to represent? Or because, however these fighters originated, by the first century AD (*pace* Gérôme) they no longer in practice used this particular piece of equipment very often? For other categories, it proves very difficult to see exactly what the difference between them might consist in. Was the Thracian the same as a '*hoplomachus*' ('shield-fighter')? Or was there, as some archaeologists try to argue, a crucial variation in the shape of his shield? Were 'Samnites' just an earlier form of the *murmillones*? And what of those categories that are mentioned in literature or on tombstones, but never seem to be represented in images? Why can we find no images of the '*essedarii*' ('chariot-fighters'), so often referred to in written sources?

A telling case is one of the most startling and now most frequently reproduced images of any fighter in the arena: a unique bronze *tintinnabulum* (bell chimes) from Herculaneum, cast in the form of a gladiator attacking his own elongated penis which is half-transformed into a panther or wolf. Leaving aside the difficult questions of where this nightmarish creature might have been displayed, by whom and why – it is a favourite object among modern historians, who want to illustrate the complex identity of the gladiator, and especially the dangerous ambivalence of his sexuality, a subject we shall return to in Chapter 4. In killing the animal, this fighter will castrate himself. 'There is no more apt icon for the Roman cosmology of desire, and the place of the gladiator within it,' as one writer has recently put it. But is he a gladiator at all, in the strict sense of the word? His headdress certainly bears little resemblance to that in other images of gladiators. Maybe we should better see him as one of the beast hunters in the arena, a much less common subject of ancient art or literature. Or maybe – and this would fit with his strangely dwarfish physique – he is meant to be a theatrical or mime artist. For all his fame in modern accounts of gladiatorial combat, he is a classic illustration of just how hard it is to pin images of gladiators down.

The fact is that modern accounts which list and illustrate the different gladiatorial types plus their characteristic weapons, and define their particular roles in the arena ('the usual tactics of the *secutor* were to try closing in on his adversary's body with his shield held in front of him', and such like), are at best over-zealous attempts to impose order on

11. The Freudian fighter? This set of chimes presents an unnerving image of self-castration. But is the figure, as many modern writers assume, really meant to be a gladiator?

the wide diversity of evidence that survives. Different types of gladiators with different names there certainly were – but how exactly each one was equipped, what particular role they took in the fighting and how that differed over the centuries of gladiatorial display throughout the whole expanse of the Roman empire is very hard indeed to judge.

The question becomes even more tantalizing when we try to fit into the picture the authentic items of gladiatorial armour that still survive – splendid helmets, shields, protections for shoulders and legs (or perhaps arms: to be honest, it is not always clear exactly which part of the body the makers had in mind). There is a considerable quantity of this, most of it, about 80 per cent, from the gladiatorial barracks at Pompeii, excavated in the eighteenth century. At first sight, even if it is not from the Colosseum itself, this material provides precious direct evidence of what an ancient combatant in that arena would have worn, only a few years before the monument's inauguration. And it matches up reasonably well with some of the surviving ancient images of gladiators. Yet it is far too good to be true … quite literally. Most of the helmets are lavishly decorated, embossed with figures of barbarians paying homage to the goddess 'Roma' (the personification of the city), of the mythical strongman Hercules and with a variety of other more or obviously appropriate scenes. It perhaps fits well with Martial's emphasis on the arena's sophisticated play with stories from classical mythology that one of these helmets (illustration 12) is decorated with figures of the Muses. It is also extremely heavy. The average weight of the helmets is about 4 kilos, which is about twice that of a standard Roman soldier's helmet; the heaviest weighs in at almost 7 kilos. Add to this the fact that none of them seem to

12. A pristine helmet from the gladiatorial barracks at Pompeii, displaying figures of the Muses. On the right perhaps Euterpe, with a wind instrument in her right hand; next to her Urania – holding a globe suggesting her connection with astronomy.

show any sign of wear and tear – no nasty bash where a sword or a trident came down fiercely, no dent where the shield rolled off and hit the ground. It is hard to resist the suspicion that these magnificent objects were not actually gladiatorial equipment in regular use.

Some archaeologists, predictably, have tried very hard to resist that suspicion, and have resorted to some desperate arguments in the process. Maybe this Pompeian armour was a new consignment, not yet knocked around in the arena. Maybe the short length of the gladiatorial bouts meant that such weight of equipment was manageable for these fit men; it was not, after all, like fighting a day-long legionary battle. Maybe – and this is where desperation passes the bounds of plausibility – the helmets were known to be so strong that no canny opponent would have bothered to take aim at them, hence their apparently pristine state. Maybe. But much more likely is that this armour was the display collection, used only perhaps when the gladiators paraded into the arena at the start of the show (to be replaced by more practical equipment as soon as the fighting started), or on other ceremonial occasions. It was the also the kind of equipment that would best symbolise the gladiator on funeral images or other works of art. Our guess is that what the spectator would actually have seen in the Colosseum or any amphitheatre was probably much less like the figure re-invented by Gérôme (who almost certainly had seen the Pompeian finds), and much more like the more lightly clad, though still recognisably 'gladiatorial', gladiators envisaged by de Chirico in the 1920s and the rather more nifty fighters depicted in the casual graffiti from Pompeii (illustrations 13 and 14). There is little reason to think that the gladiators regularly lumbered around the arena

13. De Chirico's near naked gladiators (1928) hint at an eroticised image of gladiatorial power and allure.

in their display kit (which would certainly have allowed no Russell Crowe-style balletics). Perhaps no more reason than to imagine that British university students regularly wear on campus the mortar boards, gowns and imitation fur in which they are dressed for those ceremonial graduation photographs, treasured in their parents' photo albums.

But what, finally, of the standard programme of displays in the amphitheatre: animal hunts in the morning, executions at midday, gladiators in the afternoon (with the public gladiatorial dinner the evening before to allow the punters to study form)? It is quite true that each of these elements is referred to by ancient writers describing the shows. The question is whether or not it is right to stitch all these references together into a 'programme'. This is a trap modern students of Roman culture often fall into: pick up one reference in a letter written in the first century AD, combine it with a casual aside in a historian writing a hundred years later, a joke by a Roman satirist which seems to be referring to the same phenomenon, plus a head-on attack composed by a Christian propagandist in North Africa; add it all together and – hey, presto! – you've made a picture, reconstructed an institution of ancient Rome. It is exactly this kind of historical procedure which lies behind modern views of what happened at a Roman bath or at the races in the Circus Maximus, or at almost any Roman religious ritual you care to name. And it lies behind most attempts to reconstruct the shows in the amphitheatre too.

Why is it usually assumed that the lunch interlude was the time for executions? Because the philosopher Seneca writing in the mid first century AD, before the Colosseum was built, in a letter concerned with the moral dangers of crowds,

14. These graffiti from Pompeii tell the story of three fights that took place at the nearby town of Nola. In the first a veteran Hilarus wins ('v' for '*vicit*') against a fighter who is nevertheless let off with his life ('m', '*missus*' meaning 'discharged'). Below a new boy, Marcus Attilius ('t' for '*tiro*' or novice) defeats first Hilarus, then Lucius Raecius Felix (both of whom are spared, '*missi*').

complains that the midday spectacles in some shows he had attended were even worse than the morning. 'In the morning men were thrown to lions and bears, at noon to the audience,' he quips. And he goes on to deplore the unadulterated cruelty, while explaining that its victims are criminals – robbers and murderers. That is the only evidence for the lunchtime executions (apart perhaps from a passing reference to 'the ludicrous cruelties of midday' in Tertullian's Christian attack on Roman spectacles). In fact, there is just as much evidence for some kind of burlesque or comedy interlude at lunchtime. And that may have been what Seneca was expecting, when he writes that he was hoping for some 'wit and humour'.

Why is it believed that gladiators regularly had a public meal the night before their show? Because a couple of Christian martyrs in the arena at Carthage in AD 203 were given 'a last supper which is called a "free supper"'; because Tertullian again, rather puzzlingly, claims that he himself does not recline in public 'like beast fighters taking their last meal'; and because Plutarch writing at the turn of the first and second centuries AD claims that although gladiators are offered expensive food before their shows, they are more interested (understandably we might think) in making arrangements for their wives and slaves. Maybe that is enough evidence to suggest a regular public, pre-show banquet; maybe not. There is certainly no evidence at all for the punters coming along to study form; in fact, we have no direct evidence at all for widespread betting on the results of this fighting. That is an idea that comes mostly from the imagination of modern historians, trying to make sense of the shows by assimilating them to horse racing, or to ancient chariot racing, which certainly did attract gambling.

Of course, the success of public spectacle depends, in part, on the audience having a general idea of what is going to happen. In that sense there must have been some shared fore-knowledge of what was likely to be involved in shows in the amphitheatre: animal hunts, executions, gladiators, plus (on a very lucky day) more adventurous displays such as those mock naval battles. Certainly there is a quite a lot of evidence for the animal hunts often being scheduled in the morning (it might have been easier to keep the gladiators hanging around than the animals); and casual references to 'the morning shows' do usually seem to refer to the hunts and other animal displays. But success also depends on novelty and surprise. We must reckon that, rather than the rigid order of ceremonies often assumed, the performances at the Colosseum varied enor-mously according to the ingenuity of the presenter, the amount of money at his disposal, the practical availability of beasts, criminals or gladiators. After all, a hundred days of spectacles with executions each lunchtime would surely have soon exhausted the supply of condemned men and women, even in a society as brutal and cruel as Rome. These games must have been the same *and different* each time.

The Colosseum and its shows are the most familiar part of ancient Roman culture in the modern world. Films and novels, as well as serious scholarly accounts, present to us a relatively consistent picture of the performances in the amphitheatres. At the same time as we puzzle at the cruelty and the bloodshed involved, at *why* they did it, we feel rela-tively confident that we know roughly *what* it was they did.

Most readers will be able to close their eyes and conjure an image of the Colosseum in full swing. That is why it is such an important monument in the history of modern engagement with ancient Rome. This chapter has tried to suggest that some of that confidence is ill placed. It is much harder than we often imagine accurately to recreate the scene in the killing fields of the Colosseum; still harder (as the extraordinary series of poems by Martial prompts us to reflect) even to begin to understand what it was the Romans themselves saw in this slaughter.

But happily, looking closer at the Colosseum is not only a matter of discovering that we know less than we thought. The next chapter will turn a shrewd eye towards some of the Colosseum's cast of characters: from the gladiators again, through the lions to the emperor and audience, and to what we can tell of their reactions to what they witnessed. Of course, these were only part of the cast list. Apart from a handful of references on tombstones and other inscriptions to slaves and ex-slaves who looked after the costumes or guarded the gladiators' weapon store, the vast slave battalions who serviced the building and its entertainments, the cleaners and gate-keepers, the wardrobe-mistresses and the odd-job men, are now completely (in the old catch-phrase) 'hidden from history'. Nonetheless, if we change the focus of inquiry slightly and ask rather different questions of the evidence we have, we discover that we know more than we thought rather than less.

4

THE PEOPLE OF THE COLOSSEUM

'HEART-THROBS OF THE GIRLS'?

Gladiators were marginal outsiders in Roman society. Some of them literally so: captives of war, the poor and destitute who saw in possible success in the arena their only (desperate) hope, slaves sold to the gladiatorial 'training camps' (in Latin *ludi*, usually rather too domestically translated as 'schools'), condemned men sent there as punishment. They were, in fact, almost exclusively men. Apart from a few exceptional and usually scandalous cases – such as the emperor Nero's reputed display of an entirely black troupe of gladiators, women and children included – female gladiators are more a feature of modern over-optimistic fantasy than Roman practice. The body of a Roman woman found in London in 2000 and eagerly identified as a female gladiator, on the basis of some lamps found with her carrying gladiatorial scenes, was probably nothing of the kind but just an 'ordinary' woman buried with her favourite trinkets, if anything a fan rather than a contestant.

A gladiator's life was dangerous, painful and probably short – even if for the skilled or lucky few success might bring rewards and eventually discharge. It is significant that the most famous doctor of the Roman world, Galen, who ended up as the court physician to the second-century emperor Marcus Aurelius, started his career treating gladiators in Pergamum (in modern Turkey). He claims to have found the experience useful in his studies of human anatomy and various therapeutic methods and regimes, and he drew on it in writing his voluminous medical treatises. When we read his account of the problems of replacing intestines hanging out through a gaping wound, we are probably getting close to some of the real-life gladiatorial experience in the arena. The simple presence of a doctor, however, hints at the economic interests that may have mitigated the physical conditions experienced by most of the fighters. A dead gladiator was an expensive gladiator. Likewise mangy specimens were probably no crowd-pullers. Their living quarters, clothing and rations must have varied enormously through the many different troupes and camps in the empire: some were small private-enterprise affairs (much like that of the gladiatorial impresario Proximo, played by Oliver Reed, in *Gladiator*); others were effectively part of the imperial state organisation in Rome itself, located conveniently close to the Colosseum. But, wherever they were based, logic suggests that they would not have been kept in starvation. Some Roman writers refer to standard gladiatorial fare as '*sagina*', 'stuffing' – a characteristically snobbish disdain for humble food, and at the same time hinting unpleasantly at the similarity of the fighters to dead animals. But coarse diet or not, it would probably have been eyed enviously by large sections of the Roman poor.

Beyond the physical dangers they faced, gladiators were marginalised in a civic and political sense. Many were of slave status anyway, which meant that they had only the most limited legal and personal rights. But even those who were by origin freeborn Roman citizens suffered a whole series of penalties and stigmas when they became gladiators, which in many respects amounted to losing their status as full citizens. It involved much the same 'official disgrace' ('*infamia*' in Latin) as prostitutes and actors suffered by virtue of their profession. We know of Roman legislation from the first century BC that prevented anyone who had ever been a gladiator from holding political office in local government; they were also not allowed to serve on juries or become soldiers. Even more fundamentally they seem to have lost that crucial privilege of Roman citizenship: freedom from bodily assault or corporal punishment. Roman civic status was written on the body. Part of the definition of a slave was that, unlike a free citizen, his body in a sense no longer belonged to him; it was for the use and pleasure of whoever owned it (and him). A gladiator fell into that category, as the notorious oath said to have been sworn by recruits when they entered the gladiatorial camps proclaimed. Its terms no doubt varied from place to place, but Seneca quotes a version that has a gladiator agreeing on oath 'to be burnt, to be chained up, to be killed'. Such a promise of bodily submission was completely incompatible with what made a free Roman citizen free.

It is hardly surprising then that gladiators are often treated as the lowest of the low in Roman literature, and symbols of moral degradation. Not for ancient Rome the modern political heroisation of Spartacus, the first-century BC gladiator who led a, temporarily successful, rebellion of slaves against their Roman oppressors and has starred in countless modern novels, movies, ballets, operas and musicals

– most recently in 2004 a French blockbuster show *Spartacus le Gladiateur*, who 'dreamed of being free'. By contrast, Roman politicians looking for a slur to cast on their rivals would often reach for the term 'gladiator'. And Seneca again, when writing a rather pompous philosophical essay in the form of a letter of condolence to a man who had just lost his young son, attempts to cheer him up by reminding him of the boy's uncertain and possibly ghastly future: he might have squandered his wealth and ended up as a gladiator. It is hardly surprising too that we know of repeated attempts by the Roman authorities legally to prohibit senators from fighting as gladiators in the arena.

But this prohibition should give pause for thought. For if the gladiators were so completely despised and abominated, why on earth would legislation have been necessary to prevent senators from joining them? One answer is that these regulations were more symbolic than practical. The function of law is often to proclaim the importance of boundaries, rather than literally to prevent people crossing them. The reason most of us do not commit incest is not, after all, that there is a law against it. Here we might be seeing another instance of Roman insistence that there was a firm line to be drawn between fighters in the arena and civilised (especially elite) Roman society.

There is, however, plenty of evidence to suggest that gladiators were as much admired and celebrated as they were abominated. Far from just flirting with the idea of gladiatorial combat, some members of the Roman elite did enter the arena; even some emperors (admittedly 'bad' ones) left the imperial box in the Colosseum and joined in the fight – as we shall see later in this chapter. The admiration of the gladia-

15. Spartacus, the most glamorous gladiator ever and freedom fighter *avant la lettre*, here stars in Khachaturian's Soviet ballet *Spartacus* (in a production at the Royal Opera House, Covent Garden, in 2004). The end of the story is that Spartacus was resoundingly defeated by the Roman legions.

tors took a variety of forms. While philosophers such as Seneca might with one breath deplore the degradation of the gladiators or their corrupting effect on the crowd, with the next they were seeing in the arena an example of true courage, of a 'philosophical' approach to death, even a model for how the truly wise man should act. More generally Roman households seem to have been littered with images of gladiators, combat and equipment. The lamps with gladiatorial decoration buried alongside the woman from Roman London are only one example among thousands upon thousands of such objects, from the elegant to the kitsch: not just the expensive mosaic floors or paintings with scenes of the arena (though there are plenty enough of them decorating up-market houses all over the empire), but ivory knife-handles carved as gladiators, lamps moulded in the shape of gladiatorial helmets, even, from Pompeii, a baby's bottle with the image of a gladiator in full fight. And this is not to mention the signet rings, the glass beakers, the tombs, marble coffins, water flasks, candlesticks – all displaying characters from the arena. How any of this relates to the odd custom of Roman brides parting their hair with a spear that had been dipped into the blood of a dead gladiator is frankly a mystery. It may anyway have been more a piece of anti-quarian folklore than a regular practice, as puzzling and quaint to the Romans as it is to us. One of the Roman schol-ars who did puzzle over it came up with various possible explanations. Perhaps the union of the spear with the gladia-tor's body symbolised the bodily union of husband and wife. Perhaps it was supposed to help her chances of bearing brave children. Who knows?

The strongest image of the gladiator in Roman culture,

however, was as a virile sex-symbol. Graffiti from Pompeii, probably written by the gladiators themselves (and so a boast as much as a comment), call a Thracian by the name of Celadus (or 'Crowd's Roar') 'the heart-throb of the girls' and his partner Cresces (perhaps 'Bigman', a *retiarius*) 'lord of the dolls'. It was in fact a standing joke at Rome that women were liable to fall for the heroes of the arena. The satirist Juvenal, writing around AD 100, famously turned his wit on a senator's wife, Eppia, who had apparently run off with a sexy thug from the Colosseum:

> What was the youthful charm that so fired Eppia? What
> was it hooked her? What did she see in him that was worth
> being mocked as a fighter's moll? For her poppet,
> her Sergius
> was no chicken, forty at least, with one dud arm that
> held promise
> of early retirement. Deformities marred his features –
> a helmet-scar, a great wen on his nose, an unpleasant
> discharge from one constantly weeping eye. What of it?
> *He was a gladiator.* That makes anyone an Adonis;
> that was what she chose over children, country, sister,
> and husband: steel's what they crave.

The joke here is, of course, on the woman, satirised for an insatiable sex-drive that leads her to abandon everything for this brute. This is Roman misogyny speaking loud and clear. But the last line of this extract hints at a telling pun. 'Steel's what they crave'. The Latin is *'ferrum'* – literally 'iron', or 'sword'. Another common Latin term for sword (and one embedded in the word 'gladiator' itself) was *'gladius'* – which was also Latin street-talk for 'penis'. The point about the gladiator is that he was, for better or worse, as one modern historian has aptly put it, 'all sword'.

Juvenal is satiric fantasy. But similar stories, true or not, were told of historical figures too. The empress Faustina, for example, wife of the philosopher-emperor Marcus Aurelius and mother of the notorious Commodus, was rumoured to have conceived Commodus during an affair with a gladiator. One particularly lurid ancient account claims that when she confessed this passion to her husband, he consulted sooth-sayers who recommended that he have the gladiator killed; after this he was to make his wife bathe in the dead man's blood and then have sex with her. The story goes that he followed these recommendations, and then brought Commodus up as his own son. Historians have, under-standably, been dubious about this tale, and guess that it was invented to provide a convenient explanation for Com-modus' obsessive enthusiasm for the arena.

A notorious find from Pompeii is often seen as positive confirmation of the fondness of upper-class Roman women for rough gladiatorial trade. In the excavations of the gladia-tors' barracks, the skeleton of a heavily jewelled lady came to light – presumably, it has often been suggested, caught in the act with her paramour, trapped for eternity (as every adul-terer's nightmare must be) in the wrong place at the wrong time. If so, she was taking part in a very squashed session of group sex. For in this tiny room were found not only the rich lady plus partner, but no fewer than eighteen other bodies, children included, plus a variety of bric-à-brac, chests with fine cloth and so forth. Much more likely we have the remains of a group of people fleeing the city with their prize possessions who had taken refuge in the barracks when the ash and pumice rained too hard, never to re-emerge. But if this turns out to have been no adulterous tryst after all, it is still the case that in the Roman imagination the gladiator was a figure of larger-than-life sexual power.

How then do we account for these conflicting images? How do we explain why a figure of such social and political stigma was also the object of admiration and fantasy? All kinds of ideas have been canvassed. In part we are no doubt dealing with a common fascination of elite culture for its opposite: a combination of *nostalgie de la boue* and Marie Antoinette playing at milkmaids (or, for that matter, female members of the British royal family cavorting around London clubs dressed up as policemen). In other words, gladiators were not sexy and exciting *despite* being beyond the social pale, but *because* they were. Maybe also, in a highly militaristic culture such as Rome, gladiatorial combat played a special role. Whether the Romans were engaged in active military combat or not (and long before the first century AD fighting normally took place miles from the centre on the remote frontiers), the lust for battle was replayed in – or displaced into – the arena, and military prowess found its expression in the skill of the gladiators; this could not simply be abominated. Even more important, though, must have been the power of the spectacle itself. To be the centre of attention of a vast crowd is always empowering. Hence, for example, the almost heroic status of the condemned criminal in early modern Britain giving his gallows speech in front of those assembled to watch his hanging; and hence, in part at least, the celebrity of modern football stars. To be watched by tens of thousands of people in the Colosseum, to have all eyes on you, transcended the invisibility of social disadvantage. Emperors realised this as well as anyone: when they left the imperial box to take their place in the arena, it was partly a gambit to recapture the gaze of the crowd. The emperor always risked being upstaged by the abominated creatures whom everyone was watching.

Yet there was more to the allure of the gladiator than the familiarising image of the modern footballer might suggest. The gladiator was a crucial cultural symbol at Rome because he prompted thought, debate and negotiation about Roman values themselves. Of course, there is something tautological about that claim: all crucial cultural symbols prompt negotiation about their society's values; that's what makes them 'crucial cultural symbols' in the first place. Nonetheless, gladiators and gladiatorial combat do focus attention on many of the 'jagged edges' of Roman culture: on the question of what bravery and manliness consist in; on power and sexuality; on proper control of the body; on violence and death and how to face it. Their position in Roman society, and in the Roman imagination, was bound to be contested and ambivalent.

Or so it must have been from the point of view of the audience, and of those Romans who quaffed their wine from gladiator glasses, or sealed their letters with a gladiator signet-ring. What we are missing (apart from some blokeish boasting on the part of Celadus and Cresces and the occasional ghoulish bon mot on a tombstone) is the point of view of the gladiators themselves. There is no account from any arena fighter of what it felt like on the other side of the barrier that separated the spectators from the slaughter. The hints we get, however, suggest terror was as powerful a feature as heroism. This is presumably the message of

Symmachus' twenty-nine Saxons who pre-empted the agony and humiliation of the performance by strangling each other. Even this is rather upstaged by a tale told by Seneca of another arena performer, an animal hunter, not technically a gladiator. The man, a German by birth, went off to the lavatory just before the show ('the only thing he was allowed to do without surveillance'); there he grabbed the stick with a sponge on the end (which was the Roman equivalent of lavatory paper) and rammed it down his own throat, suffocating to death. Seneca treats this as an instance of consummate courage ('What a brave man! How worthy of being allowed to choose his own death!'). We might detect desperation and terror, as well as bravery.

But Romans too could, on occasion, envisage the fearful plight of the arena fighter. In one of those strange rhetorical exercises through which budding Roman orators practised their skills, by arguing different sides of imaginary legal cases, the student was asked to plead on behalf of a rich young man who had been captured by pirates, sold to a gladiatorial troupe and later disinherited by his father. A polished version of this survives (rather like the 'fair copy' or crib of a modern school exercise), with a tear-jerking section describing the man's initiation into the arena:

And so the day arrived. The populace had already gathered for the spectacle of our suffering, and the bodies of the doomed had already been put on display throughout the arena leading a procession that was their own death march. The show's presenter who was hoping to curry favour with our blood took his seat ... One thing made me an object of pity to some of the audience – the fact that I seemed unfairly matched. I was doomed to be the

sacrificial victim of the arena; no one did the trainer hold in
lower regard. The whole place was humming with the instru-
ments of death. One man was sharpening a sword, another was
heating strips of metal in a fire [these were used to check that a
gladiator was not faking death]; birch-rods were being brought
out from one side, whips from another ... The trumpets sounded
with the wail that presaged my death, stretchers for the dead
were brought on – my funeral procession was being arranged
before my death. Everywhere there were wounds, groans and
blood; all I could see was danger.

But then, in true rhetorical style, fate intervened. A friend of
the young man appeared and bought him out, by offering
himself to the trainer instead. That was fiction; reality must
often have been more severe.

SOME DEADLY STATISTICS: AN INTERLUDE

Exactly how much more severe? How soon after they entered
the arena did most gladiators die? How many lived into honourable retirement? We get very different impressions from
the surviving evidence. Some tombstones commemorate ex-
gladiators dying in their beds (or so we guess) at relatively
ripe old ages, leaving behind loving wives, grieving children
and a clutch of slaves. There is other evidence too that some
gladiators were skilled survivors. There are some evocative
graffiti from Pompeii which record the results of bouts at
various shows, as well as the past 'form' of the gladiators concerned. We find an interesting selection of different styles of
contest: classy bouts between experienced fighters (a 15-fight
man vs a 14-fight man; 16 vs 14 and so on), newcomers

pitched against each other; the occasional newcomer versus an old-timer. But what is really surprising (although it may be more boasting) is that a handful of fighters have over fifty contests to their credit. That said, there are are a good number of memorials to gladiators who died young. A man called Glauco, we are told on his tomb, fought seven bouts and died in the eighth, aged 23 years and 5 days. His wife Aurelia and 'those who loved him' put the monument up, quoting the dead man's words: 'My advice to you is to find your own star. Don't trust Nemesis [the goddess of Vengeance]. That is how I was deceived.'

This is haphazard information and much of it comes from outside the city of Rome itself (as always, the evidence is skewed towards Pompeii and we can only assume that, writ large, it would apply to the Colosseum too). But if we put together all the evidence from Rome and the rest of Italy about the gladiators' life-expectancy – tombstones and graffiti – we do get a clearer glimpse into the frequency of gladiators' fights and their chances of survival into something approaching old age. In fact some expected and unexpected conclusions emerge. The average (median) age at death of gladiators as noted on tombstones was 22.5 years. Of course, gladiators who got such a commemoration were probably an exceptional bunch. They had to have a spouse or a comrade who cared about their deaths sufficiently to set up and inscribe a memorial, which cost cash. In general terms the sample is likely to be biased towards the successful. Even so there is a striking contrast here with the life expectancy of 'normal' Roman males. Supposing (and it is only a guess) that gladiators entered the arena around the age of 17; then, on the basis of these figures, they could expect to live just another 5.5

years. Normal males at age 17, on the other hand, had a life-expectancy of 31 years; that is, their average age at death, if they lived to be 17 (a big if: infancy would have killed off most), was 48. Unsurprisingly perhaps, even for these successful gladiators, the chances of dying early was very high.

The tombstone records are revealing in other ways too: we know that Glauco died at 23 after 8 fights; another gladiator died at 27 with 11 fights; another at 34 with 21. These figures suggest either a late age of starting a gladiatorial career, or perhaps more probably – but also more startlingly – a low frequency of fighting, at least among elite gladiators. Assuming a starting age of 17, and assuming also that they were in continual gladiatorial service up to their death, we must reckon something under two fights a year. Were gladiators afraid to fight? More likely, their owners were reluctant to have them risk death. The second-century AD philosopher Epictetus tells us that gladiators belonging to the emperor had been known to complain of not being allowed to fight often enough: 'they pray to god and pester their overseers to let them fight'. It makes a wry image to think of gladiators strenuously training every day and putting on practice bouts perhaps with wooden weapons – while fights for real were relatively rare. Though not always. In some of the biggest imperial shows (where demand perhaps outstripped the number of gladiators available) we know that individual fighters would sometimes enter the arena more than once. We saw (p. 51) that this was implied by the 'half pairs' noted in the inscriptions commemorating Trajan's blockbuster in 117. Likewise the man who came to Rome from Alexandria, probably for later shows celebrating Trajan's success (illustration 10, p. 62), fought at least three bouts in the same series:

the inscription explains that after his first bout ever, his second came just seven days later; something then took place 'at the same games', but as the text frustratingly breaks off at that point we do not know what that 'something' was – perhaps the fight that killed him.

So what were the chances of death in each fight? The figures from Italy are sparse, but suggestive, and again probably biased to the relatively successful. They under-represent the cheap 'extras' (gladiators sometimes referred to in Latin as 'gregarii', the 'chorus' or the 'B-team'), who would surely have been likely to die sooner. One set of graffiti from Pompeii gives information on 23 bouts with 46 fighters: 21 gladiators won outright, 17 were let go without penalty and 8 were killed or died from their wounds. The sample size is ridiculously small, but it is almost all we have and it implies a death rate of about one gladiator in six in each show. This roughly fits with another index of the scale of slaughter. Notwithstanding the occasional veteran with more than fifty fights to his name, if we count up all those living gladiators from Pompeii whose fight record we know, only a quarter had over ten fights' experience. Three-quarters had died before completing ten fights, implying a cumulative loss of about 13 per cent per fight. Gladiatorial combat, as Gérôme pictured it, with left-over corpses strewing the Colosseum's arena must have been an expensive rarity. In fact the emperor Augustus had banned the luxury (in Roman terms) of shows in which all fights were to the death. Not that the regulation was universally obeyed: an inscription honouring a man in a small Italian town boasted: 'over four days he put on 11 pairs, and of these he had 11 of the best gladiators in Campania killed, and also 10 bears cruelly'.

We can push these conclusions a little further, if we bring into the picture one more piece of evidence from the late second century AD, about a hundred years after the Colosseum was built. It is all very speculative and the calculations get rather more complicated, but that is part of the fun. At the time, it seems, aristocrats in the Roman provinces were becoming extremely worried about the cost of putting on shows (which was part of the duty of local magistrates). The central government, under the emperor Marcus Aurelius, intervened in 177, abolishing the tax on the sale of gladiators (reluctantly perhaps as the treasury netted a considerable amount from it) and fixing, or attempting to fix, the maximum prices which presenters in the provinces paid for gladiators. Surviving inscriptions give us the detailed terms of this legislation, all amounts in which are expressed in the standard unit of Roman currency, the sesterce. Five hundred sesterces was sufficient to feed a peasant family on minimum subsistence for a year; 2000 sesterces was the notional price of an unskilled slave. 1 million sesterces was the amount of wealth necessary to qualify for senatorial rank. The figures in the decree of 177, combined with what we have already seen about rates of death, allow us very roughly to estimate the total empire-wide expenditure on gladiators (excluding the big shows at Rome) and to estimate how many gladiators all the shows in the empire consumed.

The law divides gladiators into different pay bands. It insists that half the gladiators used in each show should be 'chorus', the maximum price for these chorus members being 1,000–2,000 sesterces each. By contrast, skilled gladiators were priced much higher, at ten levels ranging from 3,000 to 15,000 sesterces each. All the same the pyramid of differential seems low. Opera divas today, to say nothing of football superstars, get paid fantastically more than the chorus or the pack. Perhaps these low differentials reflected the high chance of death (it was not in the owners' interest to pay a fortune for a star with limited life expectancy) or a low skill pyramid (were the stars really that much more expert at this brutal game?) or, of course, the producers' desire to contain the costs.

At the same time total costs for the acquisition of gladiators at each provincial show were put into five price bands, ranging from 30,000 to 200,000 sesterces – small beer indeed when compared with the metropolitan shows in the Colosseum, which were of a quite different order of grandeur (compare, for example, Hadrian reputedly spending 2 million sesterces on a show before he became emperor – though that cost would also have included beasts, gifts to the crowd and so forth). If we imagine a relatively cheap show of, say, 60,000 sesterces and remember that half the gladiators had to be 'chorus', that would mean twenty-four gladiators: twelve chorus and twelve stars. And even if a provincial grandee spent the maximum 200,000 sesterces and put on forty gladiators (twenty chorus, twenty stars), he could still afford only two bouts between stars of the highest grade if each gladiator fought only once (and even putting them back in the ring would not greatly increase the number of star bouts, unless he made the same pairs fight each other more than once). If these regulations were followed, all provincial shows must have been small shows.

The decree of 177 also tells us that the tax on the sale of gladiators had yielded between 20 and 30 million sesterces a year for the central government, levied at either 25 or 33 per cent of the price (the decree is unclear on both points). The total price of the gladiators traded in the empire each year was, as declared for tax purposes at least, between 60 and 120 million sesterces. If we work within the coordinates we have, simplified as they must be (half of all gladiators were chorus, one in six died at each show), we can tentatively work out how many gladiators there must have been in the Roman empire as a whole and how often shows were put on in provincial venues.

Given what we know, with half the gladiators fixed as chorus, and assuming a reasonable distribution between all ten grades of star, 16,000 gladiators traded among show-presenters would have cost the bottom figure of 60 million sesterces. Is this the right order of magnitude, for provincial shows which featured normally between twenty and forty gladiators each? The answer depends on balancing the number of shows there were in a year, the number of venues, the number of fights a gladiator undertook each year and the rate of death. If we take the number of amphitheatres firmly known (over 200), add over a hundred other venues, especially in the eastern empire, which were adapted for gladiatorial shows, plus a few more for luck (to take account of gaps in our knowledge), we can guess a total of 400 venues. Allow them to stage two shows a year with an average of thirty gladiators who each fought twice a year – this was an enterprise which could all have been launched with an initial army of 12,000 gladiators. But 12,000 gladiators (400 venues × 30 gladiators) would have generated 2000 deaths in the first show and 2000 more in the second. The total throughput of gladiators empire-wide would have been 16,000. In other words, it fits!

We have taken no account here of gladiators being sold between shows (which would have added to the treasury's profits), of tax evasion, disobedience to the law, of changing patterns over time (some scholars, on not very good evidence, have claimed that the shows became crueller in the second and third centuries), or of other factors such as replacement costs caused by retirement of gladiators. It is all a very rough estimate. But some of the implications are striking. First of all, we must be dealing with very few shows in each venue per year. On our calculations, most amphitheatres, those iconic glories of Roman cruelty, luxury and profligacy, must have been empty, or used for something tamer, on 360 days out of 365. The functions of all those thousands of gladiatorial images must in part have been to memorialise and keep in the mind events that in real life were rather few and far between. Spectators were likely to have been much more familiar with gladiators practising than fighting in 'real' combat. On the other hand, 16,000 gladiators outside the capital amounts to roughly the manpower of three legions of the Roman army. Added to that, however, must be the many who were based in Rome itself (Pliny claims that before the building of the Colosseum, under Caligula, there were 20,000 in the imperial training camps – only two of whom, apparently could look danger in the eye without blinking!). We are then dealing with a gladiatorial machine perhaps equal to something like a quarter of the strength of the Roman legions combined.

What, finally, of the toll in casualties? In individual contests, as we have stressed, slaughter was far less common than our popular image suggests. But what of the aggregate of deaths in the arena? At a death rate of one in six, we have already estimated 4000 gladiatorial fatalities per year outside Rome. We need to add to that the condemned criminals executed at the shows and the deaths, accidental or not, among animal attendants and hunters; say 2000. The figures for the casualties in Rome itself are harder to estimate, partly because of the enormous fluctuations between years which saw vast displays hosted by the emperor and those when only the regular shows of senators were laid on. It may be reasonable to guess that the capital on average saw something like one third of the deaths in the rest of the empire; say 2000 again. A grand total of 8000 deaths in the arena a year is then our best tentative guesstimate. Not much of a burden, one might initially think, for an empire with a total population of 50 to 60 million people. But, in fact, 8000 deaths per year, mostly of trained muscular young adult males, would be equal to about 1.5 per cent of all 20-year-old men. Seen in these terms, the death of gladiators constituted a massive drain on human resources. Gladiatorial shows were a deadly death tax.

LIONS AND CHRISTIANS

Whatever the death rate of gladiators in the Colosseum, it must have been much worse for the beasts which took part in the shows. There were many more animals than humans involved in the arena displays – both killed and killing. For the big spectaculars at least, the practical arrangements for their capture, transportation and handling must have demanded time, ingenuity and personnel far beyond the acquisition and training of the gladiators. Not for Romans the tame pleasures of a modern zoo, safe entertainment for young children and indulgent grandparents (though who knows if some perhaps did visit the animals kept before the show in the Animal House near the Colosseum). Their chief pleasure was in slaughter, either *of* the animals or *by* them. Sophisticated this may sometimes have been, in elegantly constructed settings, rocks and trees appearing in the arena as if from nowhere, or tableaux of execution cleverly mimicking (as Martial evokes) the stories of mythology. But it is hard to see how the end result could have been anything other than a morass of dead flesh. As we saw, Dio's total of animal deaths at the shows opening the Colosseum was 9000, and 11,000 at Trajan's shows in 108–9. Even if we suspect exaggeration on the part of either emperor or historian, and even if (as must be the case) these lavish spectacles were the exception rather than the norm, there can be no doubt that we are dealing with, for us, an uncomfortable amount of animal blood.

16. A medallion celebrating the 'munificence' of the third-century emperor Gordian III. On the left of the Colosseum is the Colossus and the 'Meta Sudans' (Domitian's monumental fountain); on the right a portico appears to abut the building; inside, animals fight.

It seems that animal hunts and displays often took place in the morning of a spectacle, conducted by a special class of trained hunters and animal handlers. Though not gladiators in the strict sense of the word (and without the charisma of gladiators in Roman culture), these *venatores* and *bestiarii* ('hunters' and 'beast men') were almost certainly drawn from the same underclass, slaves and the desperate poor. One of the training camps in Rome was called the Morning Camp; and it was here, we guess, that these men were trained for the job. Part of their act was to lay on animal displays, the cranes battling cranes, for example, which Dio reported among the highlights of the Colosseum's opening, or what appears to be a fight between a bull and a mounted elephant on a coin of the early third century, showing the Colosseum. Part was more straightforward hunting. To judge from surviving images in paintings and mosaics, marksmen mostly on foot, but some on horseback, picked off the animals with spears, swords and arrows. It is hardly too fanciful to imagine that graffiti on one of the marble steps in the Colosseum itself, showing scantily clad spearmen rounding up some hounds and chasing or taking aim at a group of bears, represent what the doodling artist was watching, hoped to see or fondly remembered as taking place in the arena (illustration 17).

Most ancient writers assume that the outcome of these contests was death for the animals (and presumably in the process for some of the hunters); in fact when listing the total carnage, they tend to note the number of gladiators who *fought*, but the animals which were *slain* (suggesting that survival was an option for the former, but not for the latter). Modern scholars have occasionally flirted with the idea that some of these acts may have been 'exhibitions', in the sense that the animals survived. In fact one idea has been that a particular rhinoceros extolled by Martial for its victory over a bull at the inaugural Colosseum games is exactly the same animal as a rhinoceros mentioned in a later book of Martial's poetry, written under the emperor Domitian, *and* none other than the rhino commemorated on some coins of Domitian. He was an animal star, in other words, with several bouts to his credit, much on the lines of star gladiators. Maybe. But we cannot help thinking that a degree of modern sentimentality is creeping in here – although the sheer trouble and expense of acquiring such rare specimens might always have made saving their lives for future appearances a prudent economic move.

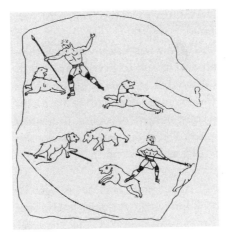

17. Graffiti from the Colosseum itself depict the contest of spearmen and animals.

The accounts we have of the animal hunts and shows always lay most stress on the fierce and exotic. In the middle of the first century BC, the great general Pompey (Rome's answer to Alexander the Great until he was defeated in civil war by Julius Caesar) is said to have laid on, amongst other creatures, twenty (or seventeen depending on who you believe) elephants, 600 lions and 410 leopards. The emperor Augustus, in his autobiography, boasts of 'finishing off' a combined total of 3500 animals in 'African beast hunts' in the course of his reign (according to Dio, this included thirty-six crocodiles on one occasion). One notoriously unreliable late Roman historian let his imagination run away with him, we must hope, when he listed the animals shown by the emperor Probus in the Circus Maximus ('planted to look like a forest') in the late third century AD: 'a thousand ostriches, a thousand stags, a thousand boars, then deer, ibexes, wild-sheep and other herbivores'. On a fantastical variant of the usual procedure, the people were said to have been let in to take what animals they wanted. The same emperor, on another occasion, is said (by the same historian) to have put on a rather disappointing show in the Colosseum. It included a hundred lions which were killed as they emerged sluggishly from their dens, and so 'did not offer much of a spectacle in their killing'.

The logic of these shows is clear enough. Whether fact or fiction, the killing (and the tales told about it) vividly dramatised Rome's conquest of the (natural) world. It would, for example, have been hard to watch the slaughter of Augustus' crocodiles without reflecting on the fact that Egypt had just been brought under direct Roman control. But the practicalities of handling all these animals must surely baffle us. This is partly a question of managing these dangerous creatures in the arena itself. Even if not when it

18. This mosaic from North Africa shows a condemned criminal (naked and held by his hair by a 'guard' in a tunic) facing a murderous lion. Not as in the comforting ancient story of Androcles, famously adapted by G. B. Shaw: there the lion remembers an earlier kindness of his human victim, who had once removed a thorn from his foot, and refuses to attack him.

first opened, the Colosseum was eventually equipped with an elaborate system of hoists and cages, which could have delivered animals from the basements, through trapdoors into the arena. But it is hard to imagine how the big animals could have been reliably controlled with the strings and whips that are shown on most of the surviving visual images. Maybe that would have been sufficient for the sort of animals that we suspect made up the regular fare at the Colosseum, the ones ancient and modern writers and artists are much less interested in: the goats, small deer, horses and cattle, even rabbits. With the large and dangerous specimens of the celebrity occasions, things could and did go nastily wrong. Pompey's elephants, for example, caused all kinds of problems in the Circus in 55 BC. The crowd reputedly much enjoyed the elephant crawling on its knees (its feet wounded too badly for it to stand up) snatching shields from its opponents and throwing them up in the air like a juggler. But it was hardly such fun when the beasts *en masse* tried to break out of the palisading that enclosed them. It caused, as Pliny remarks in a disconcertingly deadpan way, 'some trouble' in the crowd.

It is even more amazing to contemplate the organisation and expertise that must underlie the acquisition and transport of these wild animals. True, if we think of the more run-of-the-mill shows, then probably the animals could be supplied by local livestock markets – and some emperors apparently kept a herd of elephants just outside Rome, under the charge of a 'Master of the Elephants'. But – that apart – how were the more impressive and exotic victims obtained? The scale of the problem of animal procurement can be gauged by a single comparison. In 1850 a young hippo was brought to western Europe, the first for more than a thousand years, and caused a great stir in London, where it ended up in the Regent's Park Zoo under the name of Obaysch. It took a whole detachment of Egyptian soldiers and a five-month journey from the White Nile to transport it as far as Cairo. A specially built steamer equipped with a 2000-litre water tank took it from Alexandria to London, accompanied by native keepers, two cows and ten goats to provide it with milk. Compare that with the five hippos, two elephants, a rhino and a giraffe killed (according to an eye-witness account) by the emperor Commodus himself in a single two-day exhibition in the late second century AD.

How did the Romans do it? How did they capture the animals in the first place, without the convenient aid of the modern tranquillising dart? The answer seems to be by a variety of traps and pits and the cunning use of human decoys dressed up in sheepskins! And how did they manage to get these fierce and no doubt frightened creatures delivered from distant parts of the empire to the capital alive and in good fighting condition? Sceptics will answer that they often did not. Symmachus, after all, was disappointed with his emaciated bear cubs and maybe more corpses arrived than living animals. All the same, behind the exaggeration and the failures that are not trumpeted in ancient literature, the stubborn reality remains that on occasion at least large numbers of these beasts did make it to Rome. Private enterprise and personal arrangement played their part. In the late 50s BC, as we know from his surviving letters, Cicero, the new governor of the province of Cilicia (in modern Turkey), was being badgered to get hold of some panthers for shows of his disreputable friend Marcus Caelius; Cicero was evasive, claim-

'You're right. I was a fool to have given in to those damned animal-rights activists.'

19. A modern variant on the Christians vs Lions 'joke'.

ing that the animals were in short supply. But later it seems that state requisitioning of animals also made use of army detachments. It was perhaps a convenient way of keeping the troops occupied while on peacetime garrison duty. We know from inscriptions, for example, of a 'bear-hunter' serving with the legions on the Rhine and of fifty bears captured in six months in Germany.

Animals were not only brought to the Colosseum in order that they themselves should be killed. They were also used to kill criminals and prisoners in the executions that took place in the arena as part of the shows. One notorious form of execution was 'condemnation to the wild beasts' ('*damnatio ad bestias*'), where prisoners, some tied to stakes, were mauled and eaten by the animals. This is the fate to which Christian prisoners were often sentenced and is the origin of all those novels and films which take as their centrepiece the clash between 'Christians and Lions', not to mention the series of sick jokes along the lines of 'Lions 3, Christians 0'.

The fact is that there are no genuine records of any Christians being put to death in the Colosseum. It was only later (as we shall see in Chapter 6) that Christian writers invested heavily in the Colosseum as a shrine of the martyrs. No accounts of martyrdoms there are earlier than the fifth century AD, by which time Christianity had become the official religion of Rome; they look back to the conflicts between Christians and the Roman authorities centuries earlier. It is likely that Christians *were* put to death there and that those said to have been martyred 'in Rome' actually died in the Colosseum. But, despite what we are often told, that is only a guess.

One of the possible candidates for martyrdom in the

Colosseum is St Ignatius, a bishop of Antioch (in Syria) at the beginning of the second century AD, who was 'condemned to the beasts' at Rome. His writings, and those of other Christians describing death in the arena, not only offer a different perspective on the amphitheatre from the point of view of the victim, but also show how important that ideology of victimhood was in the community of the early church. Of course, we know next to nothing of the actual death experience of Christian martyrs, but Ignatius' letters, apparently written to the community of Christians in Rome on the journey to the city for his death, are full of highly charged, and blood-curdling, anticipations of the moment. He was going to his death voluntarily:

> *Let me be fodder for the wild beasts; that is how I can get to God. I am God's wheat and I am being ground by the teeth of wild beasts to make a pure loaf for Christ ... What a thrill I shall have from the wild beasts which are ready for me ... I hope that they will make short work of me. I shall coax them to eat me up at once, and not hesitate, as sometimes happens, through fear. Forgive me, I know what is good for me ... Come fire, cross, battling with wild beasts, wrenching of bones, mangling of limbs, crushing of my whole body, cruel tortures of the devil, only let me get to Jesus Christ.*

What is astonishing in Ignatius' letter is the degree to which he and his intended audience internalised 'pagan' ideals about death in the arena and subverted them to their own ends. The cruelty and suffering of the arena are now idealised as instruments of believers' salvation.

St Ignatius' letter is not an isolated example of Christian

fixation with the arena. From the second century onwards Christians created a new genre of literature, known as 'Martyr Acts', which celebrated the capture and trial (often before a capricious pagan judge) of a steadfast Christian who was willing to suffer terrible tortures and death rather than give up his or her faith. Hugely embellished no doubt, they acted as a kind of sacred pornography of cruelty, tying the Christian message to gruesome and gory death at the hands of the Roman authorities. One of the most vivid and shocking is the account of the martyrdom of two female saints, Perpetua and Felicity, at the beginning of the third century AD in Carthage. After the narrative of their trial and imprisonment, the story turns to their final moments in the amphitheatre. They were brought out, at first naked and tied up in nets, to face 'a mad heifer which the Devil had prepared'; their male friends had faced leopards, bears and boars. But, apparently, even the crowd was horrified at the sight of the two young women, one of whom – Felicity – had just given birth, her breasts still visibly dripping milk. So they were taken off, dressed again in tunics and sent back to the arena. Tossed and crushed, they nevertheless remained alive, until the crowd demanded their execution in full view. Perpetua's killer was a novice, and – despite the agony caused by his mishits – she guided his sword to her throat. 'O most valiant and blessed martyrs. Truly you are chosen for the glory of Christ Jesus our Lord.'

How far this and other such accounts are in any sense eye-witness description is a moot point. They claim to 'tell it how it was', but almost every element in the depiction is tinged with Christian symbolism and a Christian message. The bloodshed is treated as a second baptism; Perpetua (as a good modest Christian woman) does not forget to pull down her tunic when the heifer has lifted it to expose her thigh; and so forth. What is certain is that the Martyr Acts are at once an apparent rebuttal of Roman savage sadism, yet at the same time they exploit its seductive appeal. Vulnerable young women, cruelty and wild animals were as much weapons in the triumph of Christianity as in the attempt to suppress it. There can be no doubt whatsoever that the amphitheatre was the setting for dreadful violence inflicted on innocents; but it may have been a more cheap-skate, tawdry, even (if this is possible) amateurish kind of violence. Our modern image of the larger-than-life cruelty of the arena is, in part at least, a product of two very different types of investment in such a picture: the boastful exaggeration by Roman emperors and the boastful denunciation by Roman Christians.

THE PEOPLE ON PARADE

It is the first rule of any spectacle that the audience is as important an element as the display itself: we go not only to watch, but to watch other people watching, and to be seen watching ourselves. The audience is part of the show. In the case of the Colosseum, the biggest amphitheatre in the Roman world, the role of the audience was even more loaded than usual. As many recent studies have insisted, the serried ranks of the Roman people, seated in hierarchical ranks according to status, were in effect a microcosm of the Roman citizen body. This was much more extreme than the social segregation of modern spectacles, where the front seats go to those who can (and choose to) pay for them, but may equally well include those who have saved up for months for a special treat as those who would never sit anywhere else. The basic, official rule in Rome, at least by the end of the first century AD, was that civic status determined where you sat. Senators sat closest to the arena in the front rows; behind them the next official status rank of Roman society, the 'knights'; and so on up to the top of the seating area (what in a British theatre would be called 'the gods') reserved for slaves, non-citizens – and women, apart from the state priestesses known as the Vestal Virgins, who sat with the senators in the front. The senators, and maybe the knights too, sat on movable seats; the rest were on fixed benches of either brick faced in marble or, at the very top, in wood. Relegating the women to the back probably ensured that, amongst the elite at least, the audience was overwhelmingly male: no woman of any social pretensions was likely to relish sharing this distant viewpoint with the great unwashed.

Exactly how and when this detailed stratification of the audience had developed is hard to pin down (though it was certainly mirrored in other Roman entertainment venues, such as the theatre). Nor is it certain how carefully it was policed. But ancient writers certainly tell warning – or sala-cious – stories of what was likely to develop if this kind of segregation was not in place. One of the most bloodthirsty dynasts of the first century BC, Lucius Cornelius Sulla, was reputed to have picked up (or to have been picked up by) his wife Valeria at a gladiatorial spectacle, 'when the seating was not yet separated'. It is a tale rather reminiscent of the modern story of brushing up against a would-be partner in a row of cramped cinema seats. According to his biographer Plutarch, she walked behind the place where Sulla was sitting, as she made her way to her own; resting her hand on his shoulder, she removed a piece of fluff from his cloak and followed this up with some witty flirtation when he looked a bit taken aback. After the predictable collusive glances, longing looks and knowing smiles, a proposal of marriage followed: 'he was seduced' carps Plutarch, 'by looks and languishing airs, through which the most disgraceful and shameful passions are naturally excited'. But all that was officially off the menu once the regulations were introduced.

An idea of the complexity surrounding the question of who sat where comes from an extraordinary set of Roman priestly documents. A prestigious Roman priesthood, the Arval Brethren ('the Fraternity of the Fields'), over centuries of the Roman empire kept a record, inscribed in stone, of their activities, decisions and privileges. It is a unique and sometimes surprising document of what Roman priests did and what Roman religious ritual entailed; in AD 80 it included a record of the seats allocated to the priesthood and their various dependants in the newly opened Colosseum. The allocation specifies the particular block (accessed by one of the corresponding seventy-six numbered public entrance-ways into the amphitheatre, still numbered on the monument), the level of the seating from the front and the row number. The priests were not allocated numbered seats, but roughly 130 Roman feet of seat space in all (the Roman measure was a little shorter than the modern one). Different ranks among the priests and their hangers-on would presumably have occupied places at different levels in the building. So, for example, the allocation specified 42.5 Roman feet spread over eight rows of level one, in block 12; and almost 64 feet in block 53 of the top tier, spread over 11 rows.

No entrance tickets to the Colosseum survive, but we have examples from elsewhere and they must have existed: small tokens of wood, bone or lead, specifying (to judge from the details of the Arvals' seating) the block or entranceway, level and row number. So far as we know spectators did not pay for their tickets; attendance was one of the perks of citizenship. But how they were distributed is not clear. Given that everything in ancient Rome, 'free' or not, had its price, then we should probably imagine that people paid for membership of clubs and societies to which free tickets were issued. Or men of influence, powerful patrons, distributed tickets to their dependants and clients. When they arrived at the Colosseum, spectators would find that the entrance and exit routes for different classes of seating were planned (as we shall see in the next chapter) in a complex pattern so that citizens of different status were kept rigidly separate. Roman snobs did not like to rub shoulders with the less privileged, even if they were squashed side by side with their equals.

Squashed they sometimes were, at least behind the ranks of the elite on the front rows, with their much more ample individual seating. We know from lines etched into the stone benches in other Roman amphitheatres that the average space allocated to ancient spectators was only 40 cm. This is less than the space given to economy passengers on a cheap airline. We also know from elsewhere (no seats survive in the Colosseum itself) that the seatback-to-seatback leg-room averaged 70 cm. Probably Romans were on average slimmer than modern couch-potatoes; they were certainly shorter (adult males on average only 165 cm, or about 5 feet 5 inches). Even so, if the Colosseum broadly followed the space allocations known elsewhere, when it was full most spectators must have been close packed together. It was perhaps this over-close proximity that made the audience a volatile group – as when a riot broke out in the amphitheatre in Pompeii between the home crowd and the people of the neighbouring town of Nuceria and prompted the authorities in Rome to ban gladiatorial shows there for ten years.

Modern writers – ourselves included – have often laid enormous stress on the political stratification and collective identities paraded in the Colosseum audience. The spectators were a microcosm of properly regulated Roman society, sitting in their official Roman costume (the emperor Augustus, a stickler for restoring or inventing traditions, had insisted that all citizens attend shows in a toga), with the highest ranks occupying the best seats in the front and so on up to the slaves and women at the back. They acted out the social order in a 'political theatre'. This is true – up to a point. But it can be over-stated. For in other ways the audience in the Colosseum displayed the ambivalences of Roman political status and the impossibility of fitting the messy realities of the Roman population into neatly ranked status groups. Part of this is the universal problem that it is always impossible to decide which the best seats in the house really are. The senators may have had a premier ringside position. But, that said, the oval shape and the steep raking of the amphitheatre gave everyone a goodish view, provided that the fight did not end up against the wall of the arena. Besides, if shade and a view of the audience below was what you most valued, then the upper seats might seem much more attractive. For the awnings that were spread over the building to keep off the fiercest heat of the sun only protected the top half of the seats when the sun was at its zenith;

the largest area they could possibly have covered given a structure of linen, ropes and wooden ribbing is around 10,000 square metres, roughly half the auditorium. Unless they brought their own parasols or wide-brimmed hats, prestige at the ringside carried a price in sweat and sunburn.

But Roman society did not fit as easily as we often like to imagine into straightforward vertical status groups and the seating in the Colosseum probably blurred the legal distinctions as much as reinforcing them. Was it only the senators who sat in the ringside seats? Or could they bring guests and clients? Did some slaves actually sit at the front with their elite masters, or did the senators pay for their exclusivity by having to do without their everyday attendants at the ringside? We do not know the exact area of the senatorial seating (there is no precise archaeological indication of how far it extended), but the best guess would suggest that it offered space for 2000 spectators, assuming that they had twice as much space as the people in the squashed rows behind. There were only about 600 senators, and many of those would have been out of Rome at any one time (commanding the army, governing the empire). We are left with one of two conclusions. Either senators in practice occupied about eight times as much space as the ordinary citizen, which even by Roman standards of inequality seems extreme. Or seating in this area was in practice socially mixed, not just senatorial sons, but friends and contacts too.

There were other factors which would upset the neatness of the stratification of the Colosseum and other groups who found a place in its system, cutting across the official hierarchy. Fragments of inscriptions, for example, have been discovered which originally identified collective seating for 'boys' and probably also for their tutors (who, though usually slaves, would have presumably sat near their charges); another marks out space for 'citizens of Cadiz'. It seems very probable that other groups such as official delegations, artisans or traders from big cities acquired the right to sit in particular places, whether by favour or purchase, quite separately from their formal place in the legal hierarchy. In the later empire, individual aristocrats had their names carved in marble to indicate their personal or family seating space. The Colosseum was not, as is sometimes implied, simply a place where the political collectivity of Rome was on view; it displayed individual variance, power and influence too.

And what proportion of that collectivity would be included in the audience anyway? Almost no one now believes the late Roman account which seems to suggest that there were 87,000 seats in the Colosseum; at best, it has been argued (though for no particularly strong reason), this really meant 87,000 feet of seating space, not individual seats. Modern estimates cluster around an estimated capacity of about 50,000. But Rome in the first century AD is thought to have had a population of one million, which suggests some 250,000 adult male citizens. On this reckoning, even when it was completely full, the Colosseum would have held only one fifth of those citizens, and even less in that some space was taken up by women, boys, slaves and outsiders. Our guess is that, even though the shows were free, the poor and the very poor were systematically under-represented (as they are in most social benefit systems in any place or at any period). If this is correct, the audience at the Colosseum was more of an elite of white toga-clad citizens than the rabble proletariat often imagined today.

The emperor was the sponsor of the most spectacular shows in the Colosseum, which he watched in the presence of his people from the imperial box in a prominent position at the centre of one of the long sides of the arena's oval. Ancient writers devote so much attention to the emperor's role at these Colosseum shows that it is now hard to recapture any image of the monument without the imperial presence or to recover any information on shows that were sponsored by 'ordinary' aristocrats. That is partly the point. For the Colosseum quickly became one of the key contexts (if not *the* key context) in which the emperor's quality and worth were judged.

'Good' emperors were defined as such by their behaviour in the arena: they generously showered the audience with presents or tokens that could later be exchanged for yet more valuable objects; they offered lunch (or at least the ancient equivalent of a cheeseburger and Coke in their seats) to the onlookers; they never ever looked bored with what was going on, never used the privacy of their box to get on with some paperwork, but they did not take too much pleasure in the shows either (a difficult tightrope to tread, no doubt, between disdain and fanaticism). They also sprang witty surprises. It was presumably in the Colosseum that an emperor in the middle of the third century AD, Gallienus, played an ingenious trick on a man who had sold his wife glass jewels instead of real gems. He is supposed to have ordered the man to be taken off as if to be thrown to the lions, but when the cage was opened, a capon tottered out. The emperor had his herald proclaim to the astonished audience, 'He practised deceit and had it practised on him.'

'Bad' emperors were just the opposite. Typically they were supposed to transgress the boundaries on which the logic of the shows rested, most obviously by turning themselves into gladiators and the audience into victims. The notorious emperor Caligula, in the mid first century AD, about fifty years before the Colosseum itself was built, is said to have been so short of criminals for execution that he had some of the spectators thrown to the beasts instead. Domitian, among others, had members of the Roman elite fighting as gladiators. But it was the emperor Commodus who offers the most vivid case of the intersection of the emperor's image with gladiatorial combat.

Commodus was assassinated in AD 192, by a lethal consortium of his mistress, chief chamberlain and commander of the guard. They had supposedly discovered his plans to kill them all, which the emperor had carelessly left written on a wooden tablet, when he fell into a drunken sleep after lunch. Besides, Commodus was also said to have been planning on the very next day, 1 January 193, to murder the consuls and present himself as holder of this traditional office dressed not in a toga, but as a Roman gladiator, emerging to meet the people not from the palace but from the gladiatorial training camp where he had lodgings. True or not, it is the closest we ever come in Roman history to the image of the emperor being, as it were, completely re-branded as a gladiator. And it goes along with all kinds of other evidence for the promotion of the figure of 'emperor-as-gladiator' during Commodus' reign. He is supposed to have fought hundreds of gladiatorial bouts himself (in private, it was said, these were fights to the death, or at least he clipped off a few of his opponents' noses; in public it was display bouts only, with wooden swords and no bloodshed). According to a late scandal-mongering biographer, which may at least reflect rumour at the time, he had the great statue of the Colossus altered so that it bore his own features, and his titles inscribed at the base of the statue included two new imperial sobriquets: 'Gladiator' and 'Cross-dresser' (in Latin, '*Effeminatus*'). When he was assassinated, the gleeful acclamations of the senate apparently included the refrain 'Cast the gladiator into the charnel house'.

The most extraordinary account of Commodus' exploits in the arena comes from the historian and senator Dio, who was himself an eye-witness to many of them from his ring-side seat in the Colosseum: 'I was there myself and I saw and heard everything and took part in what was spoken; so I have thought it right to suppress no details, but to hand them down just as they happened, just like anything else of the greatest weight and importance.' On one occasion, Commodus opened the extravaganza by killing a hundred bears with spears, throwing them from specially constructed walkways which divided up the arena. As Dio implies, this was more a demonstration of accuracy than courage – but even Edward Gibbon, whose tart denunciation of these antics in the Colosseum is a marvellous set-piece in *Decline and Fall*, was forced to concede that 'some degree of applause was deservedly bestowed on the uncommon skill of the Imperial performer'. The next day he killed some relatively harmless domestic animals, some of which were in nets in any case (just to be on the safe side presumably), plus a tiger, hippo and elephant. That was a morning's work. In the after-noon he fought a demonstration bout as a gladiator, armed with a shield and wooden sword, against an opponent armed only with a wooden pole. Unsurprisingly, Commodus won, and then settled down to watch the real bouts – some of which he oversaw from a platform in the arena, dressed up as the god Mercury.

Dio insists that when the emperor was fighting, the senators and knights always attended. Only one principled character stayed away, who would rather have died (literally) than be forced to watch all this or join in the chanting that was required of the elite: 'You are lord, and you are first, and the most blessed of all. Victor you are, and victor you will be …' The common people, however, had more choice than their betters and were much more inclined to give the proceedings a miss, partly out of disgust, partly because they had heard a rumour that the emperor was planning to shoot some of the spectators, in the guise of Hercules shooting the Stymphalian birds. (This must have been one of those occasions when even an imperial blockbuster in the Colosseum was not playing to a full house.) Not that the senators were any less anxious. Dio in fact describes one particular unforgettable incident which panicked as much as it disgusted and amused the senators in the front rows. Commodus had just killed an ostrich in the arena and cut off its head. Approaching the senators in the audience he held up the ostrich head in his left hand and a bloody sword in his right and, without speaking, grinned at them – as if to say that he would or could do much the same to them. 'And,' to quote Dio's exact words, 'many of us would have died by the sword there and then, for laughing at him (for it was laughter not indignation that took hold of us), if I had not myself chewed on some laurel leaves which I picked from my garland, and persuaded the people sitting near me to do the same, so that we might conceal the fact we were laughing by the steady movement of our jaws.'

In this story, the Colosseum is the setting for one of those very rare occasions when we can, almost physically, empathise with the Romans. We know exactly what that laugh of Dio's – caused by a mix of hilarity and sheer terror – would have felt like. And most of us have vivid memories, from school if not later in life, of suppressing a giggle that would inevitably get us into trouble by biting our lips, a sweet paper, a ruler or whatever. But what on earth was going on in these extraordinary gladiatorial antics by the emperor? In part, as we suggested earlier, the arena and the gaze of the people sets up a competition for popular attention between emperor and performers. It is one of those awful ambivalences of Roman imperial power: the emperor sponsors the show, but always risks being upstaged by the *déclassé* stars of the fighting; yet he is bound to humiliate himself if he decides to direct the people's gaze to himself by usurping the position of the fighter. The Colosseum was, in other words, a venue that is central to the emperor's image as benefactor of his citizens, but one in which he found it hard to win. In part too, as Dio's tale of the ostrich head waved in front of the senators must hint, the arena provided a context for the display not so much of the Roman collectivity, but of its conflicts and fissures. The bitter rivalry between aristocrats and emperors is a leitmotif of Roman history. And yet there they were, staring at each other across the Colosseum. It is hardly surprising that the two sorts of conflict (fighter versus beast; emperor versus senate) were repeatedly intertwined, that one infected the other, that one was used as a means of fighting the other. In

[117]

short, the Colosseum dramatised the emperor's struggles with himself and with his rivals.

VIEWS AND COUNTER-VIEWS

What, finally, did the spectators think of what they saw in the arena? Modern accounts tend to divide ancient reactions into far too simple categories. Most Romans (bloodthirsty culture that Rome was) did not disapprove of the shows. A few oddballs, such as Seneca, expressed their revulsion. Christians, for obvious reasons, saw in them the cruelty of Roman paganism to which they were so strongly opposed. We have already seen several reasons to query this simple picture. Martial's poetry hinted that the touchstone of approval/disapproval was not necessarily appropriate for understanding his response to the events in the arena. Despite all the Christian attacks on the institution, 'sincere' as many of these undoubtedly were, the rise of Christianity, as we have argued, was paradoxically tied to the violence of the amphitheatre. In the case of Seneca, he may have expressed his horror at the executions at midday, but he was nonetheless there in the arena (not) watching, and in his philosophical work he could use gladiatorial combat as a positive model in ethics.

The fact is that Romans (or at least the elite Romans whose words survive) were reflective about their own culture, the culture of the arena included. Their reactions to it were certainly different from our own, but there is no reason to suppose that they were any less complicated. Roman historians and anthropologists, for example, wondered about where the different elements of the shows – especially the gladiators and the animal hunts – came from and what their original function had been. They claimed to know that, long before the regular arena performances, the first display of gladiators in Rome had happened in 264 BC as part of the funeral celebrations of a leading aristocrat. This funerary connection was developed by Tertullian and other early Christian writers to suggest that this form of combat lay in human sacrifice to the spirits of the dead, thus damning its very origin with the worst religious crime of all, for Christians and pagans alike. (Despite the obviously ideological slant of this theory, modern scholars often repeat it as if it were known fact.) Other ancient writers were more interested in the geographic origins of the gladiators. A Greek historian in Rome under the emperor Augustus, puzzled by the Roman practice of sometimes bringing on gladiators at the end of a dinner party, linked it with customs in Etruria and claimed an Etruscan origin for gladiators as a whole. This has sent modern scholars scurrying off to the paintings in Etruscan tombs, where they claim (unconvincingly in our view) to have found traces of proto-gladiatorial combat. For others, both ancient and modern, Campania, south of Rome, seemed, or seems, the most likely home of the first gladiators – which fits conveniently, though not necessarily significantly, with the fact that the earliest surviving stone amphitheatres are in this part of Italy.

Romans also reflected on the ethics of the arena, with many of the doubts, ambivalences and contradictions we ought to expect. So, for example, Marcus Aurelius, Commodus' father (unless we believe that story about Faustina's gladiator lover), claimed in the sixth book of his philosophical ramblings, euphemistically known as the

Meditations, to have found gladiatorial shows 'boring'. And in 177, in his reign (along with his son Commodus as co-ruler) the legislation we used in our calculations of gladiator numbers was prefaced with one of the most striking criticisms of the cruelty of the shows that is recorded in Roman history. In abolishing the tax on the sale of gladiators, the authorities argued that the treasury 'should not be stained with the splashing of human blood' and that it was morally offensive to get money from what was 'forbidden by all laws of gods and humans'. What Commodus' attitude to this was we can only guess! But even with Marcus Aurelius himself there are odd contradictions; not least of which is the fact that in AD 175 he himself had apparently put on a massive show at Rome with 2757 gladiatorial fights. Whether we are dealing with a change of heart, political expediency, vacillating moral purpose, or a combination of all three, is impossible to know. But it certainly suggests that it is harder to pin down ancient attitudes to gladiators than is often assumed.

It is out of the question for someone in the early twenty-first century not to deplore the slaughter of the arena. In antiquity intense enthusiasm for the shows went hand in hand with a whole range of rather different ethical doubts (and snobbish expressions of disdain). Both philosophers and theologians questioned the effect on the audience of watching the bloodshed. Did it, as some argued, damage the capacity for rational thought? What was the effect on the human mind and character? St Augustine writes memorably in his *Confessions* of one Alypius, who was eventually to become a Christian bishop, going unwillingly to some shows with his friends. Though determined to keep his eyes shut, as soon as he peeped he was hooked. The spectacle had done its work:

'when he saw the blood, it was as though he had drunk deeply on savage passion'. Others wondered about the moral differences in shows involving different legal categories of victim: killing criminals was one thing, killing Roman citizens quite another. Of course, these are not our own objections; nor, in pagan antiquity at least, do they amount to anything approaching a campaign for the abolition of the shows. That said, they show the Romans thinking rather harder about these spectacles than their popular image would have it.

We have already in this chapter wondered whether the shows in the Colosseum were always quite the extravagant displays that they are painted; whether the roaring crowd did always fill every vacant seat (as the digital technology of *Gladiator* made it). We end it by wondering whether the crowd – different in their reactions as they must be from us – were quite the conscience-free and murderous enthusiasts for indiscriminate killing that it is convenient for us to imagine. True, in our terms, they were horribly cruel. Their ethical boundaries were drawn in very different places from our own; but that does not mean they had no ethical boundaries, or ethical doubts, at all.

5

BRICKS AND MORTAR

THE ORIGINAL COLOSSEUM?

It is a well-known axiom among archaeologists that the more famous a monument is, the less likely any of its original structures are to survive – the more likely it is to have been restored, rebuilt and, more or less imaginatively, reconstructed. There is an inverse correlation, in other words, between fame and 'authenticity' in the strictest sense. The Colosseum is a classic instance of this rule. A large proportion of what you see when you visit is much later than the original work of Vespasian and Titus in the 70s AD. The puzzle of dating the individual parts and the different phases has kept archaeologists amused for centuries. The truth is, though, that – despite the confident assertions of most guidebooks – it is now impossible in many cases to be certain which bits were built when. The usual euphemism that the 'skeleton' of the building is still essentially in its original form may be true enough, but it glosses over the question of how much of the building counts as the skeleton.

The monument has suffered all kinds of damage – from fire, earthquake and other natural and man-made disasters – throughout its history. There are records of repairs up to perhaps as late as the early sixth century AD, commemorated in inscriptions that have been discovered in the building (the latest one documents the restoration of 'the arena and the podium, which had collapsed in an abominable earthquake'). A particularly devastating blaze in 217 is described by Dio, who claims that the 'hunting theatre was struck by lightning … and such a conflagration followed that the whole of the upper circuit and every thing in the arena was consumed; and then the rest was ravaged by the flames and dismantled'. The building was, according to Dio, out of use for many years. But even with this clear testimony, it has proved difficult to identify exactly the third-century repairs or their extent. The most recent attempt has concluded that the damage was more limited than Dio implies, but at the same time has suggested that one section of the main outer wall of the building, usually taken to be part of the original first-century construction, actually dates from the rebuild in the third century.

The problem is that dating Roman brickwork and masonry is a tricky art. Some Roman bricks were stamped with makers' marks in the course of their production and these 'brick-stamps' can give (or allow one to deduce) an exact date. Yet, even so, it is often hard to tell whether the dated brick is part of a small repair or the main phase of construction – or even whether an old brick has been used to patch up damage centuries later. And not just in the ancient world itself. The Colosseum has continued to be repaired and adapted ever since. Some of this work used material indistinguishable from that used by Romans or, even more often, reused Roman material that was lying about the site. It is now not always possible, even for experts (though few like to admit it), to tell an eighteenth-century insertion from a fourth-century one. Of course, this sense that the monument is a patchwork of many centuries gives it much of its charm. But it also makes it hard to trace the details of its history.

The other main problem in reconstructing the original monument – whether as it stood at its inauguration in AD 80 or at any later period in the Roman empire – is the simple fact that so much of it has disappeared. True, its silhouette remains a magnificent and imposing presence in the Roman city-scape, and it is especially impressive from the air flying into the airport at Ciampino from the north (sit on the right-hand side of the plane). But about two-thirds of its ancient fabric has gone, most of that, as we shall see in Chapter 6, rifled in later periods to provide the building material for medieval and renaissance Rome. Large sections of the building as it now stands are not ancient at all, but the result of restoration over the last two centuries. Outside, half the outer wall has been destroyed; inside, there is no arena floor and no seats survive (the small reconstructed section of seating on the north-east side is a fantasy of the 1930s and gives a misleading impression of the original layout – illustration 20). Besides, the stark, almost industrial, character of the monument today is the result of the loss of almost all of its marble facings, its rich paintings and stuccoes, and the statues that once decorated the exterior arches. A relief sculpture of the Colosseum from a first-century Roman tomb gives a quite different, and probably more accurate, impression of the decorative excess of the building in its original state (illustration 21).

Nonetheless, there is still a lot to be learned from a careful look at the surviving remains. The archaeology of the building in some important respects enriches our understanding of what went on there. Equally the accounts of the shows, the gladiators and the animal hunts we have already discussed

20. The only reconstructed seating in the Colosseum is some wishful thinking of the 1930s. Also visible (bottom left) is the modern wooden flooring over part of the arena. What appears to be the wall of the arena (just below the seating) is in fact the back wall of the service corridor running around it.

21. A no doubt imaginative ancient depiction of the Colosseum. But note the entrance porch (topped by a chariot) on the left and the statues in the niches.

help to make sense of the tantalising ruin that is the Colosseum today.

THE COLOSSEUM ABOVE GROUND

However confusing it can appear on the site itself, the basic design of the Colosseum is clear enough from the ground plan (figure 1): a series of concentric circles, leading in from the vast perimeter wall to the space of the arena in the centre. The surviving section of the perimeter wall on the north side (buttressed at each broken end in the nineteenth century) is arranged in four arcaded storeys, each of which corresponds to a floor level on the interior. On the first three storeys are open archways, with half columns in three different orders of architecture, Tuscan on the ground floor, Ionic on the first and Corinthian on the second (a sequence that was admired and often copied in Renaissance buildings). The top storey repeats the Corinthian order, but has small windows rather than open arches. The total height is 48 metres, and in its original extent it is estimated to have used some 100,000 cubic metres of travertine stone, quarried at nearby Tivoli.

At the very highest level of this outer wall are the sockets which were used to attach the awning (the 'sails' or '*vela*') that served to keep the sun off the audience. (If you look up from the inside of the building when the sky is bright blue, these sockets are clearly visible.) It used to be thought – and it is still sometimes said – that the five stone bollards which survive on the ground to the east side of the Colosseum, about 18 metres away from the building, were also connected with the awning system: as if part of a series of giant tent pegs that would originally have extended all round the building and have been used to anchor the ropes of the awnings to the ground. Part of a series they almost certainly were, but they would have been disastrously ill-suited to such a weighty task, as they have no foundations and are simply bedded into the soil. A much better guess is that they played some role in a controlling visitors and access to the building.

Working in from the exterior, we find a series of four circular corridors (usually known in studies of this building as 'annular corridors' from the Latin for 'ring', '*anulus*'). These give access to different parts of the monument and to the stairways leading up to higher levels as well as offering amenities such as water fountains and, we must assume, lavatories (though, unlike the fountains, no undisputed remains of lavatories have been discovered). These annular corridors supported the structures above, constructed in a mixture of travertine, other local stone and brick. As the cross-section shows (figure 3), the number of corridors decreases as you move further up the building.

There were eighty entranceways into the Colosseum from the outside. The four at the main axes were differentiated from the other seventy-six and it is generally assumed (on some – but frankly not very much – evidence) that these were used by the performers and the emperor and his party or by the officials presenting the show. The two on the long axis to east and west are usually taken to be the performers' entrance and exit (the best argument for this is the adjacent stairs connecting them with the underground service areas of the Colosseum). Modern scholars (and ground plans) often slap technical-sounding Latin names on them: the 'Porta Libitinensis' or 'Libitinaria', after the goddess of death,

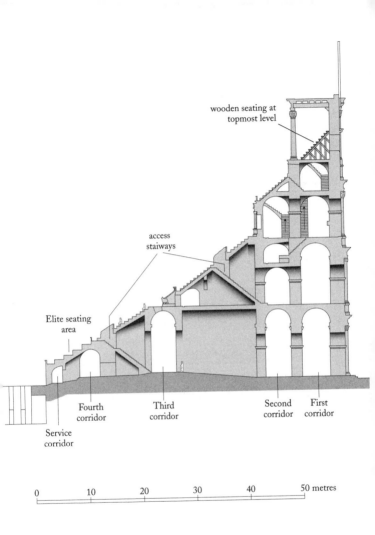

wooden seating at
topmost level

access
staiways

Elite seating
area

Fourth
corridor

Third
corridor

Second
corridor

First
corridor

Service
corridor

0   10   20   30   40   50 metres

Figure 3. Cross-section of the Colosseum (reconstruction).

Libitina, at the east, through which dead gladiators were removed; the 'Porta Triumphalis' at the west, through which the gladiators are supposed to have entered in procession at the start of the show (alternatively it is known as the 'Porta Sanivivaria' ('Gate of Life') through which the still living gladiators walked out of the arena at the end of their bout). In fact, there is almost no evidence for any of these names, still less that they were regularly applied at the Colosseum. The term 'Porta Sanivivaria', for example, is known only from the story of St Perpetua's martyrdom in Carthage; 'Porta Libitinensis' comes from a single puzzling reference in a late biography of Commodus to the emperor's helmet being twice taken out (it does not say from where) 'through the Gate of Libitina'.

Of the two entrances on the shorter axis, normally taken to be used by celebrity spectators, only that on the north survives; but the symmetry of the monument would suggest that it was mirrored on the south. There are still traces at the north of a vestibule that would once have protruded out from the line of the main exterior wall. Putting this evidence together with the first-century sculpture of the Colosseum (illustration 21) and with images on coins allows us to reconstruct a monumental entranceway on each side, topped by a four-horse chariot presumably carrying the emperor. If the Colosseum were one of the key contexts in the city of Rome for the display of the emperor, imperial statues would have been a particularly resonant and appropriate image over these two principal entrances.

Even more striking is the evidence we have for the stucco decoration at the north entrance. Although only a very few fragments are still visible, when they were much better preserved these stuccoes were drawn by Renaissance artists (including Giovanni da Udine, a pupil of Raphael, who based some of his designs for the Villa Madama on them). The exact interpretation of these is not made easier by the fact that different artists depict them rather differently – divergences that may themselves suggest that the stuccoes were not as well preserved in the Renaissance as they appear, or at least that a degree of imagination has gone into these apparently antiquarian documents. Nor is the date certain: perhaps part of the original first-century decoration, more likely part of a later makeover. But whatever they represent and of whatever date, they are precious evidence for the lavish decoration of the building that has now almost entirely disappeared. Other fragments of brightly painted plaster survive from the corridors, on the basis of which it has been tentatively suggested that vivid colours were widely used in the building's early phases, toned down to something rather less flashy later.

The main principles of the original seating plan are, as we have seen, clear enough: the seats were ranked hierarchically from the ringside to the top of the house. We can also trace on the ground plan the routes that must have led to the different areas of the auditorium (figure 1): senators, for example, would have entered and made straight for the seats on the podium at the front (Route A, and repeated round the building); those sitting at the highest level would have made straight for the stairs (Route B, repeated), without any opportunity to mingle with the aristocrats, and would then have emerged through a balustraded opening into their designated block (some of the late decorations of these balustrades survive). On the other hand, reconstructed cross-

22. The elaborate stuccoes which survived at the north entrance of the
Colosseum until, at least, the sixteenth century.

sections of the building (like our figure 3), which confidently mark the exact position of the seats and the number of rows, are based on much less firm information than their clear lines would suggest. The simple reason for this is that no seating survives and so all reconstructions are based on a more or less rough guess of what would fit on the skeleton that remains. This problem is especially acute in the elite sections of the building. The podium on which the (movable) senatorial seats rested certainly extended further down than what now appears, to a casual observer, to be the boundary wall of the arena. This is in fact the back wall of a tunnel which carried at least part of the elite seating above it (illustration 20 and figure 3) and probably acted as a service tunnel around the arena's edge – with openings through its now largely destroyed front wall onto the arena itself. But the exact extent of the senatorial area is uncertain, as is its form: it is some-times reconstructed as a sloping area, sometimes as stepped. All these uncertainties make an accurate estimate of how many people it could accommodate (p. 111) very difficult.

The most elite seating of all was in the boxes that we assume took pride of place on the north and south sides of the arena, and are regularly illustrated in imaginative versions of the Colosseum from Gérôme to Ridley Scott and beyond (illustration 8, p. 57). Nothing remains of these, but they must have been located at the ringside, approached by the elaborate entranceways at north and south. There is strong evidence to connect the position at the centre of the southern side with the emperor himself, for an underground passageway has been discovered which gave access to the ringside at this key point from somewhere outside the building to the east. About 40 metres of it has been excavated but the starting point has not been identified (figure 1). What is clear, however, is that it was an insertion (possibly under the emperor Domitian soon after the building was opened) into the original structure and that it was elaborately and richly decorated. The walls were originally faced in marble or alabaster, later replaced with frescoed plaster; there was lavish stucco on the vault and in niches; the floor was covered in mosaic. It seems very likely indeed that this passageway gave the emperor private access to his box, in addition to the main entranceway on the ground floor. In fact, its popular name is now 'the passageway of Commodus', so called after a story in Dio that Commodus was once attacked by a conspirator 'in a narrow entrance way' in the Colosseum – a nice illustration of the emperor's vulnerability even (or especially) here. If the connection is right, he would have been attacked in his own private corridor, leading to his own ceremonial seat.

If the southern box was for the emperor and his party, what of the northern box? Different scholars and different tourist guides come up with plausible, and not so plausible, ideas. Some imagine that it might have provided overflow accommodation for minor royals and hangers-on. Others suggest that this would have provided suitable accommodation for the Vestal Virgins (whom Gérôme chose to put next to the emperor). It could also have provided for magistrates, particularly those sponsoring the shows. No one knows. And, in any case, it might not always have been used by the same people, or even used at all.

Ancient spectators, sitting in any of these locations, would have enjoyed a view quite different from that offered to the modern visitor. Over the complicated web of foundations that we now see would once have been a wooden floor (not unlike the small section recently inserted by the Italian Antiquities Service (illustration 20) to help visitors more easily imagine the original appearance. The ancient flooring would have been covered with sand ('*harena*' in Latin, hence the modern word 'arena') whether to prevent slippage, or soak up the blood and the urine, or both. But the security of the spectators must have been as big an issue as the general salubriousness (or otherwise) of the fighting space. There would have been something in the order of a 4 metre drop between the senatorial seating and the arena floor, but that might seem rather close for comfort in the face of a couple of angry elephants. Almost certainly there were more safety measures in place. A graffito found during nineteenth-century excavations in the Colosseum has been (rather optimistically, we feel) interpreted as a picture of latticework balustrading around the senatorial podium; but, in any case, there must have been some kind of further barrier in that position, whether in this form or not. Roman ingenuity, however, could do better than that. The two rustics, whose visit to an earlier amphitheatre was the subject of an elegantly whimsical poem in the reign of Nero (p. 38), pick out the clever device designed to keep the animals away from the spectators. This seems to have involved sets of ivory inlaid rollers around the edge of the arena, which would prevent any animals (or vengeful gladi-ator, for that matter) getting a foothold, and an extra fence laid some way into the arena, with a net (a *golden* net in the poem) spread out from it to the podium where the elite were sitting. It is often assumed that some such devices would have been used in the Colosseum too. Much as they appreciated their ringside view, the Roman aristocracy were no doubt as keen on self-preservation as we are, and suitably cautious.

THE COLOSSEUM BELOW GROUND

Confronting the modern visitor to the Colosseum, at the heart of the building, is a mass of subterranean walls, which have been the subject of intense debate and sometimes bitter controversy since they were first re-discovered in the early nineteenth century (although it was not until more than fifty years later that any of them went on permanent display). All kinds of issues have been argued over: the date of their construction and their different phases, the exact function of the different parts and (as we explained in Chapter 3) the implications of all this for the question of whether or not the inaugural celebrations of the building in AD 80 could possibly have featured a mock sea battle. But before we explore some of the details of these arguments, and in particular the colourful controversies that seethed over a few years in the early nineteenth century, it is worth considering briefly those aspects of this subterranean world of brick masonry that are not (or not much) in dispute. For the minor details have often swamped more basic, but more important, conclusions.

What is now for us the centrepiece of the monument is 'below stage'. It is an area larger than the arena itself, if only because at each end of the major axis there are storerooms and (at the east) a corridor leading underground directly to one of the main gladiatorial training camps, with its own practice arena, known as the Ludus Magnus (literally the 'Big camp'). It is a maze of corridors and hoists which once

[136]

brought caged animals to the surface via trapdoors in the wooden floor. Stage scenery, which might transform the arena into a world of make-believe, could also be lifted in this way. It is still possible to see the rope burns in the stone edges of some of the lift wells; and archaeologists have uncovered a few of the bronze fittings which held the revolving capstans which were integral to the hoisting machinery. A clever system it certainly is (though exactly how a hippopotamus would have fitted in is hard to imagine); but this must also have been a truly horrible underground world. The maze of corridors would have been dimly lit by skylights at the edge of the arena, and elsewhere by smoking oil lamps. It does not take much imagination to see that this must have been a hive of sweating labour: slaves, skilled stage-hands, animal trainers, hunters, wild animals in their cages, chained criminals and presumably some of the gladiators, all packed together in tiny cells and passages. Above they would have heard the awful thudding of the hunts and contests. Today the noise of just tourists above, ambling across the reconstructed section of floor, is bad enough (although, as these areas are not usually open to the public, most visitors do not have the pleasure of sharing this terror). An elephant or two is hard to contemplate. This was a hell-hole.

Most of the hoisting shafts visible today date from around 300, with some later repairs. The current orthodoxy is that the original plan did not include any such system occupying the area under the arena, and that during the reign of Titus animals would have been let into the arena using hoists fixed on the perimeter wall – or even from the service tunnel under the senatorial podium. The first versions of these major substructures are generally thought now to date from the reign of Titus' successor, Domitian. But this is what the controversy has been about.

The subterranean structures first began to be systematically uncovered by Napoleon's archaeologists, working with the Pope's archaeological team, during the French occupation of Rome between 1811 and 1814; though they had not reached the bottom of the area beneath the arena before the work was stopped by flooding. Nonetheless, even these partial discoveries prompted a furious row and angry exchanges of pamphlets between leading scholars (sometimes hiding behind unlikely pen names) that were satirised in cartoons of the time. There were three main parties. The first was the papal archaeologist, Carlo Fea, who is now probably best known for producing an Italian edition of J. J. Wincklemann's *History of Art*, still widely used. Fea argued that the substructures that had been revealed were not ancient at all, but medieval, and that the original surface of the arena had not therefore been on top of these substructures, but underneath them several metres below the level of the seating; this was the only way, he argued, that it was possible to conceive of a naval battle in the Colosseum, as Dio's testimony demanded, which would not have been feasible with all those masonry insertions. Against him, an architect, Pietro Bianchi, and the Professor of Archaeology at the University of Rome, Lorenzo Re, contended that the substructures were contemporary with the original building (they were, after all, aligned with it) and that the arena floor had been laid on top of them. In support of this they pointed out that, if the fights had taken place at the low level Fea suggested, then great swathes of the arena would have been out of the line of sight of many in the audience, who would

Fieriſſimo Combattimento fra gli Antiquari di Roma nel Anno 1813
Dedicato al sig. Barone Vanderveer

23. A contemporary cartoonist captures the 'battle of the Colosseum' in the early nineteenth century. Fea stands in the water, holding up the literary texts which supported the idea that the building had been flooded for naval battles. His adversaries wield plans and inscriptions against him from dry land.

not have been able to see into what was to all intents and purposes a pit. They also relied on the evidence of the late Roman inscription commemorating the repair of the arena after an earthquake (p. 123) – for only if it had been elevated on brick and masonry supports could it have been destroyed by an earthquake. As for Dio's claim about a naval battle, he must have been wrong; Bianchi and Re preferred to follow the evidence of Suetonius who, as we saw (p. 43), located the naval battle elsewhere. The final player was a Spanish priest and antiquarian, Juan Masdeu, who tried to steer a middle path, casting himself as a 'pacifier' of the warring factions. He judged that Fea was correct on the original form of the Colosseum, but that the substructures had been inserted in the later third century and the arena floor raised to go on top of them only then. So Dio could have been right about a naval battle there in AD 80.

In many of these old archaeological arguments one suspects that, if one had been a participant oneself, one would have been on what is now seen to be the wrong side. It frankly would have seemed far more sensible to dismiss this warren of walls as a medieval insert and to imagine all the activity in the Colosseum – land- or water-based – taking place on the firm ground underneath it (after all, because of the flooding which put a stop to the excavations, Fea did not know exactly how deep the substructures went). An arena floor perched on a web of rough masonry would have seemed a very odd idea indeed. We have a strong feeling that in 1814 we would have been with Fea (just as we would probably have been with the Cambridge Professor of Greek Richard Jebb, who at the end of the nineteenth century dismissed some of the prehistoric remains excavated by Heinrich

Schliemann at Mycenae as a Byzantine slum). But whatever the strength of the arguments on all the different sides, this Colosseum controversy is distinctive for highlighting the problems of interpreting the building that have not significantly changed over 200 years. The issue still is how do you stitch together the different forms of evidence – literary, archaeological, as well as 'common sense' views of how the building must have been used – which do not actually quite fit. Can you massage away the contradictions? With all our more extensive knowledge of the structure of the Colosseum and more sophisticated archaeological dating techniques, the modern orthodoxy is still a version of the Pacifier's compromise: that the substructures are ancient, but were not in place at the very beginning of the building's history. The arena floor was elevated at its current height, but more simply – so allowing Dio's claim about naval battles to be right.

But *was* Dio right? For all the up-to-date careful analysis and new discoveries (including what appear to be patches of waterproofing on the surfaces of the cavity below the level of the arena), we still do not know. It partly depends on how grandly to interpret the spectacular Dio refers to: large boats manoeuvring on a substantial depth of water, or a rather more Toy Town affair in an overgrown paddling pool? But more than that, it depends on a good answer to the question of water supply. Even with the paddling-pool model, we are not sure how the space of the arena could have been filled with water, and drained again, at reasonable speed. One suggestion, which involves using sluice-gates and backflow water from the Tiber, would also have had the effect of bringing quantities of sewage into the arena along with the water. Hardly the image of lavish and luxurious spectacle that

Martial's poetry would have us believe. Certainly a naval battle with a difference.

PLANS AND SPECIFICATIONS

For the design of the Colosseum, water was mainly a problem in a quite different sense. It may be hard to see now how any spectacular sequences of flooding and draining were arranged for the shows. But on a day-to-day basis the pressing issue was how to prevent the Colosseum as a whole, constructed as it was in a river valley, reverting to the lake that the site had been under the emperor Nero. Besides, the building itself acts as a huge water barrel: rainfall on the seating and arena, sometimes torrential, has to be drained away, otherwise up to 175 litres of water a second would accumulate during a heavy storm. One of the most extraordinary – albeit unseen – achievements of the Colosseum's designers is to have arranged the drainage. Recent archaeological work on the water system has revealed an intricate network of underground drains, around and through the centre of the monument. The ring drain in fact runs 8 metres below the valley floor and takes the water off to flow into the Tiber. Before they even thought about the foundations, the designers had expertly arranged the site's hydraulics. Obvious as it is, this raises the question of the architectural and constructional skills necessary for such a huge enterprise. Or to put it as most visitors would when they confront this vast structure: how on earth did the Romans build it?

The usual answer is to stress the combination of vast quantities of slave labour (skilled and unskilled), long traditions of practical craftsmanship and a high level of technical and theoretical architectural expertise on the part of the principal designers. That is broadly correct. We can deduce from a minute examination of the Colosseum's structure and dimensions how an over-arching plan of considerable sophistication (though, at the same time, drawing heavily on traditional designs) was executed by teams of more or less expert workmen.

Part of the trick was to use, and adapt, relatively simple ratios and standard units. It seems that the ideal ratio of length to width for the arena itself was 5:3. According to one plausible recent reconstruction, the original plan for the Colosseum was to have an arena 300 Roman feet long by 180 Roman feet wide. The convention, as we can observe in other amphitheatres, was to make the width of the auditorium equal to the width of the arena, which would have given a total length of 660 Roman feet (300 + 360), a total width of 540 Roman feet (180 + 360) and a circumference to the whole building of 1885 Roman feet – as an architect could have calculated through relatively simple trigonometry. Did this matter? Yes, because the size of the perimeter intimately affects the design and number of the external arches. A grand amphitheatre had to have a number of grand entrances and the convention, it seems, was for the arches of those entrances to be 20 Roman feet wide (a convention that would have made it easier to instruct the artisans). The Colosseum was to have eighty arches, which – if the 20-Roman-foot standard was to be preserved and allowing for the width of the columns themselves – meant reducing the perimeter slightly, to 1835 Roman feet. This was achieved by leaving the size of the auditorium, and so of the audience capacity, intact, but reducing the size of the arena to 280 × 168 Roman feet (still in the ratio 5:3). In other words, the architects balanced the need for size and scale against the desire to work to simple and familiar ratios and intervals.

This meant that on the ground they could leave teams of artisans and their foremen with a clear plan, which would not need much hands-on supervision from the overall designer. We can see by examining the individual arches on the exterior how much the details of execution could vary from example to example. The vertical jointing patterns are quite different from pier to pier, presumably reflecting variety in the size of travertine blocks delivered from the quarries or sawn on site, and measurements that were not crucial to the overall structure could differ from arch to arch by as much as several centimetres. Likewise it seems that in the design and building of the stairways, the individual teams and perhaps under-architects had a good deal of independence. On the other hand, the voussoirs in the arches – crucial to the stability of the structure – are close to identical, and the outermost annular corridor on the ground floor is 5 metres wide and varies along its entire length by less than 1 per cent. Where it mattered, Roman architects or their design team could ensure absolute precision from their workforce.

So far, so good. But this reconstruction of the principles of working methods tends to conceal how little we know about the identity of those who designed the building: the myth about the architect being a Christian by the name of Gaudentius is just that, a myth; we have no clue who was in charge of the project. It also conceals how little we know about the methods and skills involved in the design. Despite the survival of a first-century architectural handbook by Vitruvius, our understanding of how Roman architects actually went about their work, and what the balance was between traditional practical craftsmanship and highly technical calculations of loading, proportion, lines of sight and so forth, is largely based on guesswork. We have a few traces of ground plans (preserved on inscriptions) and a handful of three-dimensional models of buildings which may have been made by architects to guide the builders on site or to inform (and please) the client. But it is very little to go on. We also read the odd anecdote about architects and their imperial clients, which make various allusions to drawings and plans, as well as to the perilousness of a design career under the emperors. It is said, for example, that Apollodorus, the emperor Trajan's favourite architect, when explaining some architectural details to his client, was interrupted by the young Hadrian. Unimpressed with the young man's architectural expertise, he told him brusquely to 'get back to his still-lifes'. Later, when he had become emperor himself, Hadrian sent to Apollodorus his own plans for a new temple, 'to show that a great work could come about without his help'. Apollodorus was predictably dismissive of the emperor's schemes and paid for his candour with his life. What the relationship was between Vespasian and Titus and their anonymous architect – whether or not we should envisage top-level meetings with the clients keenly discussing plans, sketches and models – we can only guess.

There is a sense also in which talk of ratios, units of measurement, traditional craftsmanship and slave labour makes the whole process of construction seem rather too easy. To appreciate the extraordinary scale of the labour, it is worth looking once again at the work and planning involved in those parts of the scheme that were never intended to be visible. For after the complex drainage network, before the building could ever get off the ground, came the foundations.

The Colosseum's deepest foundations are roughly in the shape of a doughnut. Under the walls and seating they are a full 12 to 13 metres deep, and – for safety's sake – this depth of underpinning continues for 6 metres outside the perimeter wall, under the pavement. Beneath the arena itself, however, the foundations are shallower, only about 4 metres deep. Simply digging the hole, an oval, about 200 metres × 168 metres and probably 6 metres deep, with pick and shovel was a huge enterprise. It seems likely that some of the excavated earth was used to raise the ground level around the whole building by about 6.5 metres, so that the new amphitheatre stood up proud in its valley setting. (The whole valley floor had already been raised 4 metres with debris from the great fire of Rome in AD 64.) The rest of the spoil from the huge hole, 100,000 cubic metres, that is about 220,000 tonnes of it, had to be carted away in ox-carts, lugging 500 kilos at a time at a speed of less than three kilometres an hour, to the port along the river Tiber. No mechanical diggers, no 30-tonne trucks; only sweat and muscle.

Once the whole area had been excavated, another huge labour began. Two great perimeter walls (one 539 metres, the other 199 metres long), 3 metres thick with a rubble core, 12.5 metres high, retained the solid concrete and rubble foundations. Once the retaining walls had been built, the remaining hole – over 250,000 cubic metres in volume – was filled with concrete, lime, mortar and sand mixed with water and volcanic rock. It is only in the last few years that archaeologists have managed to take core samples from these underpinnings and to establish their make-up and dimension. Much work remains to be done, but the main point is already clear: the Colosseum still stands because it was built on very solid foundations indeed.

Even with all this detail, the scale of the work on just this preliminary phase of construction may still be hard to grasp. In order to bring it rather closer to home we asked a firm of Chartered Quantity Surveyors to estimate the costs of creating the Colosseum's foundations in England now, at today's prices and using modern methods and materials. The specification was as follows:

The site is flat, filled with compacted clay, with good but city-centre road access.

Dig a hole 6 metres deep, in the shape of an oval (A) 198m × 178m.

An inner oval (B) on the same axes, 80m × 47m, needs to be only 4m deep.

Around the outer perimeter (A) construct a brick-faced wall with cement and rubble fill 539m long, 3m wide and 12.5m high.

Around the inner perimeter (B) construct another brick-faced wall with cement and rubble fill, 199m long, 3m wide and 12.5m high.

Fill the oval (A) between outer and inner perimeter walls with cement plus stone or broken brick to a height of 12.5m, volume 262,467m³.

Fill the inner oval (B) with cement and broken brick or stone to a depth of 4m, volume 11,772m³.

Use part of the excavated spoil (152,003m³) to raise the ground level for 40 metres outside the external perimeter wall (A) from 16m above sea level (asl) to 22.5m asl. This will use about 50,000 m³ of the spoil.

Transport the remainder of the spoil (about 100,000 m³) one hour trucking distance; include price for disposal.

Include provisional sums for cost of cement, sand, stone, timber shuttering, brick.

This is less detailed information than a modern quantity surveyor would normally require. But the provisional estimate we received, which included no drainage work, no professional fees, no VAT, nothing whatsoever above ground – not to mention those elements in the building scheme of which we are unaware or have forgotten to include – was £28.5 million. Of course there is much that cannot be compared (the use of slave rather than wage labour, for a start). None the less, this figure does give a baseline for thinking about the scale of the ancient Roman enterprise.

LIFE AFTER DEATH

THE END OF THE GLADIATORS

Modern visitors to the Colosseum may feel a sense of frustration in discovering that it is not possible to identify the great architect who designed it. Not so their medieval counterparts, some of whom at least thought they knew exactly who had been responsible for the design. For there was a strong popular tradition that the architect had been none other than Rome's greatest poet, Virgil, who was supposed to have combined his literary skills with a talent for such arts as magic, necromancy and architecture. This was a fascinating attempt to incorporate a major Roman figure into the history of a surviving monument; and it was entirely fanciful, of course – if for no other reason than that Virgil had in fact died decades before the Colosseum was built.

Not that in this tradition Virgil was supposed to have used his design skills for building an arena of deadly combat, gladiators and animal hunts. The standard medieval view was that the Colosseum was a Temple of the Sun, originally roofed with a gilded dome, and the home of all kinds of demons; and one of the favourite medieval etymologies of 'Coliseum' derived the title conveniently from the Latin word for 'to worship' (*colo, colere*). This is how *The Wonders of Rome* saw it, a pilgrim-guide originally written soon after

1000 (though this quotation is taken from a later, more elaborate edition):

> *The Colosseum was the temple of the Sun, of marvellous greatness and beauty, disposed with many diverse vaulted chambers, and all covered with a heaven of gilded bronze where thunders and lightnings and glittering fires were made, and where rain was shed through silver tubes.*

In the middle there was supposed to have been a huge statue of Jupiter or Apollo (perhaps a reminiscence of the Colossus) symbolising Roman power. The story went that when Pope Sylvester in the early fourth century had this temple of idolatry destroyed, he had the head and the hands of this statue displayed in front of what was then the principal Christian church in Rome, St John Lateran.

There were other variant medieval theories about the Colosseum. A twelfth-century English traveller known as 'Master Gregory' reported that it had been the palace of Vespasian and Titus (a brave attempt presumably to make sense of a remembered connection with those emperors). But it was not until the Italian renaissance humanists got down to work on classical texts, from the fifteenth century onwards, that the building became generally recognised again for the amphitheatre that it had originally been. Even so the connections with magic and demons did not disappear. In the sixteenth century Benvenuto Cellini, the brilliant Florentine jeweller (even if appalling self-promoter and thug), went to the Colosseum on at least two occasions by night in the company of a Sicilian priest (and part-time necromancer) in order to use the black arts to recapture his girlfriend. On the

24. This sixteenth-century painting by M. Van Heemskerck offers a glimpse of the different associations of the Colosseum, on which it is clearly based: bull-fights; a quack doctor selling his wares (bottom right); preachers; and in the centre a statue of Jupiter.

second occasion this proved a rather too successful experiment in summoning the spirits and the necromancers terrified the wits out of themselves. As Cellini explains in his *Autobiography*, no fumigations seemed effective in persuading the demons to leave – until one of the party in panic 'let fly such a volley from his breech' as John Addington Symonds' delicate translation puts it ('gave such a blast of a fart accompanied by a vast quantity of shit' is closer to the demotic Italian) that the evil spirits took to flight. In the morning Cellini and his friends made for home, not entirely certain they had escaped scot-free. In fact, a little boy in the group 'all the while … kept saying that two of the devils he had seen in the Colosseum were gambolling in front of us, skipping now along the roof and now upon the ground'.

For us, it is hardly possible to imagine the Colosseum being thought of as anything other than an arena of gladiatorial display and animal hunts. But by the eleventh century the connection of the ruined monument with its original function was a distant one. It had not been used for such spectacles for centuries: the last clear record of gladiatorial combat there is in the mid 430s; animal hunts are known to have continued for a century or so more. As late as 523 the Roman senator and bureaucrat Cassiodorus drafted a letter to a consul (responsible for staging hunts in the Colosseum) on behalf of his master, the then ruler of Rome, the Gothic King Theodoric. In it Cassiodorus deplores the cruelty and excesses of the spectacles, while lingering on their details: 'The first hunter, trusting to a brittle pole, runs on the mouths of the beasts, and seems, in the eagerness of his charge, to desire the death he hopes to avoid … The man's bent limbs are tossed into the air like flimsy cloths by a lofty spring of his body'; and so on. But Cassiodorus also makes clear that such shows were still extremely popular (even if, as usual in such accounts, there is a trace of the snobbish assumption that the populace will flock to see what their betters rightly disdain); and more to the point he drafts what is effectively Theodoric's formal authorisation of the shows, urging the consul, as sponsor, to be generous. How much later this continued, however, is anyone's guess.

It would be comforting if the end of arena spectacles could be pinned directly to the triumph of Christianity. But in fact, when Constantine, the first Christian emperor, came to power at the beginning of the fourth century, his legislation against gladiatorial shows seems to have had about as much visible effect as a thirty-mile-an-hour speed limit at the outskirts of a British town. Besides, Constantine's policy was not one of outright banning; we have evidence, for example, in an inscription from the central Italian town of Hispellum (modern Spello) that he gave specific permission in the 330s for the local people to hold annual gladiatorial shows there, apparently so that they would not have to make the difficult journey to those in the town of Volsinii. Some laws were certainly passed through the fourth and into the fifth century prohibiting various aspects of arena culture (senators, for example, were banned from using gladiators as bodyguards). But as with the edicts which during the same period outlawed paganism, the reaction was presumably a mixture of obedience, evasion and complete flouting.

In the end it was not so much the legislation (high-minded, religiously driven or not) that put a stop to the bloody spectacles in the Colosseum and elsewhere. Rather, repeated civil wars and barbarian invasions limited the capacity of the state and individuals to sponsor shows, to procure wild animals and (in the case of the Colosseum itself) to keep up a costly, high-maintenance monument. Behind the series of inscriptions which commemorate restorations of the Colosseum at this time probably lie a series of much more amateurish 'patchings-up' of an already decaying, down-at-heel, half-abandoned building than we usually imagine (and almost certainly on a smaller scale than these boastful commemorations try to suggest). In parts the building was probably already being quarried for stone in the final stages of its life as an amphitheatre. The Colosseum and its traditional activities were beyond what the resources of Rome in the fifth century could sustain. Constantine had, after all, transferred the principal capital of the empire to Constantinople (modern Istanbul), with all the funding and infrastructure that went with it. And so weakened had Rome itself been by wars, invasions and natural disasters, that the Byzantine historian Procopius estimated that (aristo-crats apart) there were only 500 people there when the Gothic King Totila invaded in 545. Of course, the terrible decline of the late antique city is almost as much a cliché as the overwhelming grandeur of the imperial capital. We should not take Procopius' figure as a good guide to the usual population of the city at the time (in addition to his likely exaggeration, many inhabitants with means and sense surely left town – as Procopius implies – in advance of Totila's arrival). Nonetheless this was not a community with either the human or material resources to keep up a monument on this scale even in moth-balls, let alone in working order.

It is perhaps no surprise then that when, on 3 September 1332, a bullfight was supposedly held in the Colosseum's arena in honour of the visit of Ludwig of Bavaria, people at the time do not seem to have made the link with the activities that had taken place there in antiquity. To us, the resemblances are uncanny: we have some more or less contemporary descriptions of bulls maddened by the blows of their human combatants, and striking out fatally at those who had wounded them; the final death toll is said to have been eleven animals and eighteen humans. To most of those watching, the connection between beast hunts and the ancient Colosseum had been forgotten.

THE COLOSSEUM REMEMBERED

The story of the lifting of this collective amnesia and of the rediscovery (or reinvention) of the monument as a tourist shrine to gladiatorial combat extends over centuries of the modern history of the city of Rome: from the feudal warfare of the medieval town, through dynastic rivalries of popes and cardinals, repeated invasions (of foreign travellers and pilgrims as much as of hostile armies), to the re-creation of the city in the late nineteenth century as the capital of a newly reunited Italy. Throughout this time, while the imperial palace on the Palatine crumbled, as Byron noted, into insignificance, while the Roman Forum gently sank under what was aptly called a 'cow pasture' ('*Campo Vaccino*'), the Colosseum still stood reasonably proud. Albeit half buried in earth itself, on a more or less greenfield site as Rome's built-up area contracted, and sometimes flagrantly misunderstood (at least by our standards), it remained one of the most striking ancient monuments of the city – rivalled only by the great columns of Trajan and Marcus Aurelius.

25. A romantic ruin or an overgrown squatter city? This late-eighteenth-
century drawing gives some idea of the build up of earth in and around what
we think of as the lower levels of the Colosseum.

We may now be thankful that some of the more breath-taking schemes for its preservation or re-use did not get off the ground. In the sixteenth century, for example, Pope Sixtus V, as *Murray's Handbook* observed in 1843, had planned the conversion of the Colosseum into a wool factory. It was a project somewhat reminiscent of those of the more enlightened British nineteenth-century industrialists and was, in fact, linked to a much bigger scheme of what we would call 'regeneration' of the area around the building. The plans drawn up by Sixtus' architect, Domenico Fontana, sited the industrial plant on the ground floor of the monument, with attached housing for the workmen on the upper levels. But the immense cost of the proposals meant that they were abandoned after the Pope's death; instead, in 1594, a small glue factory moved in. Radical as it seems, in the long term such a conversion might inadvertently have contributed to the Colosseum's better preservation (that is certainly what the French scholar Mabillon thought, when he wrote some years later that 'If Sixtus had lived, we would now have that amazing amphitheatre intact'). Not so the earlier version of Sixtus' plans, which seem to have envisaged the total demolition of the building in a major road scheme. This proposed obliteration rather exceeds the rapaciousness of later English grand tourists. 'If the Colosseum were portable, the English would carry it away' was one eighteenth-century joke. They presumably often returned home with a fragment of souvenir masonry in their pockets.

In fact the monument was repeatedly 'carried away' in a different and less damaging sense. From the Renaissance onwards, it provided a model for classicising architects. Not only was it drawn, redrawn and reconstructed on paper, it was recreated in stone – particularly the characteristic sequence of the different architectural orders on its perimeter wall. The stamp of the Colosseum is to be found in the design of many an Italian *palazzo*. As early as 1450, the renaissance architectural guru Leon Battista Alberti incorporated motifs from the building into his Palazzo Rucellai in Florence. In Rome a century later, Antonio da Sangallo, who had himself made detailed drawings of the Colosseum, replicated details in his design for the Palazzo Farnese. Sangallo's father had already taken the orders and articulation of the Colosseum as the inspiration for the courtyard of the Palazzo Altemps (just off the Piazza Navona, and now open to the public as a museum of Roman sculpture).

By the nineteenth century, imitation was as much about function as form. If the ghost of a Roman amphitheatre lies somewhere behind every circular concert hall, the very idea of the Colosseum as a place of popular Roman entertainment is paraded in all the venues world-wide that were built with that name. From South Dakota to Tokyo, there are literally thousands of sports facilities, music halls and theatres graced with the title 'Coliseum' (the spelling gives away the nineteenth-century origin of this fashion). Many of these show no trace whatsoever in their design of their Roman origins. But the London Coliseum – now the home of the English National Opera, but which started life in 1904 as a more down-market variety hall – is full of allusions to Rome, even specifically to the Colosseum itself. There are mosaics on the floors; the original carpets carried the distinctive logo of the Roman state: 'SPQR' ('Senatus PopulusQue Romanus' or 'The Senate and Roman People'); sculptures on the exterior feature some, admittedly docile, lions; and the decoration of the ceiling includes a *trompe l'oeil* version of the famous awning used to keep the sun off the spectators in the Colosseum and other amphitheatres. Sir Oswald Stoll, whose brainchild it was, is supposed to have hoped that it 'would be as worthy of London today as the ancient amphitheatre of Vespasian was of Rome'. As always with these wondrous monuments of international renown, part of their fame and familiarity stems from the fact that they have spawned replicas and creative imitations far beyond their original home.

It is now impossibly complicated to trace the precise stages by which the Colosseum was transformed in popular imagination and in popular use from a temple of demons and an arena of necromancy to a romantic ruin, a memorial of gladiatorial combat and Christian martyrdom, and an archaeological monument. In detail, its whole history since antiquity is a series of bright ideas, dead ends, failed schemes and repeated re-interpretations and re-appropriations. But the key to understanding what has happened to the Colosseum over the last millennium or so and the apparently wildly conflicting ways that it has entered Western culture is to pare those details down to their essentials. Since the end of antiquity, there have basically been just four main interest groups claiming the Colosseum for themselves: robbers and re-users; Christians; antiquarians and archaeologists; and – surprising as it may now seem – botanists. The monument's history has been largely determined by the struggles of these partisans; its changing image has been the consequence of the dominance of one interest over the others.

By the sixth century, even if it still hosted the occasional animal hunt and was kept partially in working order, the Colosseum was almost certainly in a dilapidated state. Without regular upkeep, dilapidation gave way to ruin. Its surviving structure was an obvious and easy target for those who wanted building materials, whether on a small scale (heaving off a block of travertine for use as a doorstep) or in order to provide the stuff of some of the grandest building schemes of the papal court. For most of the Middle Ages and early Renaissance the Colosseum was not so much a monument as a quarry.

To describe this activity as 'robbery' is to give the wrong impression. For the most part, there was nothing illegal or unofficial about the removal of this stone. The Colosseum's succeeding owners (a motley crew, which included feudal warlords, the local Roman council and various organisations of the Catholic Church) regularly gave or sold permission for 'quarrying'. Papal records up to the seventeenth century repeatedly include the formula '*a cavar marmi a coliseo*' ('to quarry stone from the Colosseum'). The scale of the removal is now hard to contemplate. One entry in the records notes that in just nine months in 1452 under Pope Nicholas V 2522 cartloads of stone were removed; it was apparently intended for use in lime-making in his schemes for the Basilica of St Peter's. Only a few years before, in 1448, one of the most learned humanists, Poggio Bracciolini, had ruefully observed, not without some exaggeration, that most of the Colosseum had been turned into lime. The same point was made rather more wittily in a well-known quip about the Barberini family's plundering of the monuments of classical antiquity, in particular the famous temple known as the Pantheon: '*Quod non fecerunt barbari, fecerunt Barberini*' (less neatly in English, 'What the barbarians did not do, the Barberini have done'). Papal records from the seventeenth century show Pope Urban VIII allowing this same family (of which he himself was a member) to take fallen travertine from the Colosseum for the building of their Palazzo Barberini.

Earthquakes and other natural disasters no doubt helped in this process of quarrying; with each new tremor more building material would become easily available. But, however it fell down, the great missing stretch of the main perimeter wall of the monument ended up in the architectural masterpieces of renaissance Rome. Apart from its luck in withstanding earthquakes, the surviving northern wall of the perimeter seems to have been preserved partly at least in the interests of papal ceremonial: it lay directly on the road from the church of St John Lateran (to the east of the Colosseum) to the centre of the city, one of the main routes for religious processions. Rather than plunder this impressive backdrop, they allowed the dismantling of what was then the back of the monument to the south.

There is something satisfying as well as slightly sad in the thought of stone from Vespasian and Titus' amphitheatre having a second life in the steps of St Peter's or the Palazzo Venezia (from whose balcony Mussolini famously addressed the crowds in the square below). Part of the attraction of the city of Rome is exactly this type of use and re-use, and the way the ancient city is literally *built into* the modern city that followed it. Yet there is an unsettling irony in some of the connections here: not least is the fact that several of the buildings whose design was inspired by the Colosseum were actually built with stone taken from the Colosseum. If the process had continued there would have been little left to inspire.

Ruins are not just plundered, however; they are also colonised. At the same time as stone was being removed from the site by the cartload, other parts of the building were being taken over for all sorts of domestic and commercial use. Some of this was the predictable kind of squatting. From the sixth century there are traces of animal stalls and shacks and haylofts (something of a well-deserved come-down, we cannot help thinking, for those parts of the building through which senators had once glided without having to cross the path of the lower orders). This kind of occupation continued for centuries, documented in legal records of ownership which refer to small houses, gardens, courtyards and boundary walls nestling in and around the building, and to their owners as blacksmiths, shoemakers, lime-pit workers and so forth. It was here that one early sixteenth-century artist found inspiration for an image of the Nativity, turning this shanty village into a convincing recreation of the humble stables of Jesus's birth. But it is now hard to recover much substantial evidence of these medieval settlements. The problem, as usual, is that most of the post-classical material was removed by archaeologists in the nineteenth century, who had eyes only for the classical amphitheatre and its decoration (though occasionally they mistook a medieval wall for an ancient one and preserved it!). What is left are some scattered fragments of pottery, glass and metals, and the traces of inserted partitions, patched-up floors and the predictable troughs and mangers. This farmyard air (and smell) continued well into the eighteenth century when – the grandiose industrial schemes of Sixtus V having come to nothing – a manure dump, for use in making saltpetre, was established in 1700 in the north corridors of the Colosseum. The dump remained there for a century, seriously corroding the stonework in the process.

Not all the occupation in the Colosseum was quite so down-at-heel. In the middle of the twelfth century part of the building was taken over by the so-called 'Frangipane Palace'. The Frangipane were one of the families of warlords who dominated Rome at the time. Like several others, they established their fortresses ('palace' is a misleadingly domestic euphemism) in such ancient buildings as still stood: the Colonna family took over the Mausoleum of the emperor Augustus, the Savelli the Theatre of Marcellus. It is a tradition which has not, in fact, entirely died out: there are a number of expensive private apartments, even now, in the upper floors of the Theatre of Marcellus. In the Colosseum, the Frangipane occupied a substantial portion of the eastern side – about thirteen arches in extent – on two levels. They had an extensive residence in other words, even if, we suspect, rather draughty; and for Carlo Fea, in the famous early nineteenth-century dispute (p. 138), they were the prime suspects for inserting the substructures in the arena, which he believed to be medieval. The Frangipane lost control of the Palace in the mid thirteenth century to the rival Annibaldi family, who eventually sold it in the 1360s to the Christian 'Order of St Salvator'. During their ownership, the Annibaldi are said to have entertained the poet and humanist Petrarch in the Colosseum in 1337; and they would, of course, have had a ring-side seat at that bullfight in 1332. Although disused by the sixteenth century, traces of this palace are still visible on site.

What eventually, albeit slowly, brought this re-use of the Colosseum to an end were the activities and pressure of two other groups with an interest in the building. Since as early as the fifteenth century, antiquarians had objected to the despoiling of the ancient monument. Poggio was not the only intellectual to complain of the Colosseum disappearing in the builders' carts and we shall soon turn to look at the increasingly powerful effect of this archaeological voice. But of more immediate impact in changing the culture of the Colosseum were the interests of the Christians – or rather (as, strictly speaking, almost everyone involved in this part of the Colosseum's story, from the plundering popes to the Frangipane, were Christians) that growing sense among some members of the Christian community that the Colosseum was a building of special religious significance. The place where, as they believed, so many saints and martyrs had died ought to be a hallowed place of worship, and certainly should not be tainted with bullfights, squatter occupation and piles of manure.

CHRISTIANS

On the outer face of the east wall of the Colosseum there is an inscribed plaque, put up on the orders of Pope Benedict XIV in 1750; it replaced (as it states) an earlier text painted on the walls of the building in 1675, which after nearly a century had faded. Written in Latin, it celebrated the sacredness of the Colosseum in these terms:

> *The Flavian amphitheatre, famous for its triumphs and specta-*
> *cles, dedicated to the gods of the pagans in their impious cult,*

redeemed by the blood of the martyrs from foul superstition. In order that the memory of their courage is not lost, Pope Benedict XIV, in the jubilee of 1750, the tenth year of his pontificate, had rendered in stone the inscription painted on the walls by Pope Clement X in the jubilee of 1675, but faded through the ravages of time.

This was the high-water mark of the cult of the Christian martyrs in the Colosseum. The inscription was intended permanently to define the monument as the site of the Christian victory over paganism. The year before, in 1749, Benedict had pronounced it sacred ground, dedicated to the Passion of Christ, and threatened punishment for any desecration.

There is, in fact, as we saw in Chapter 4, not a shred of contemporary evidence that any Christians were ever martyred in the Colosseum for their faith. A number of Christian accounts of the lives and deaths of the saints, written from the fifth century on, attempt to fill out and embellish the historical details by claiming that they were killed '*in amphitheatro*'. But there is no reason to suppose that the Colosseum is always meant or, when it is, that the location is anything more than plausible guesswork. More to the point, although it seems to us inconceivable that this tradition should have been completely forgotten through the Middle Ages, the standard medieval view of the building certainly did not link the Colosseum with the fate of the saints. Although other shrines associated with martyrs were keenly venerated, there is no sign of any religious appropriation here. Significantly, the pilgrim-guide to the *Wonders of Rome* picks out, for example, the Circus Flaminius (another Roman spectacle arena) as a place of martyrdom, while the Colosseum appears as a 'Temple of the Sun'.

The cult of the martyrs seems to follow directly on the reassertion by renaissance humanists of the original function of the building and their study of the classical texts that threw light on the shows and their setting. A notable fifteenth-century image in silver gilt of the martyrdom of St Peter pictures him outside the distinctive form of the Colosseum – anachronistically, as Peter was put to death years before it was built. By the seventeenth century the martyrology of the place had become a minor industry: long lists of names and dates were published, recording all those (and ever more of them) supposedly martyred there.

There were two main consequences for the monument of this growing preoccupation with its role in a specifically Christian history. First, the despoiling and dismantling began to slow down. This was neither a sudden nor a complete change. In fact, for many years the papal authorities seem to have been making money from the quarry with one hand while blessing the martyrs of the Colosseum with the other. Sixtus V, in the late sixteenth century, is a good case of such vacillation: as well as planning to demolish the building or turn it into a wool factory, he also seems to have toyed with the idea of consecrating it. At the same time the beginnings of a concern for the consolidation and the safety of the structure are visible. Substantial rebuilding started in the eighteenth century (disconcertingly for those who value original authenticity, a considerable proportion of the monument as it stands today is actually eighteenth century or later). So too did strategic demolition of fragile sections thought liable to endanger visitors and pilgrims. In the early nineteenth century, popes sponsored the two vast buttresses that still protect the 'bleeding' ends of the main perimeter wall.

The other consequence was that the Colosseum became ever more incorporated into Christian ritual, and ever more marked with Christian symbols. From 1490 until the middle of the sixteenth century a Passion play was regularly performed in the arena on Good Friday. By 1519 a small chapel of Santa Maria della Pietà had been constructed at the east end of the arena – using building material from the ancient monument, of course. Plans by the architect Gianlorenzo Bernini in the 1670s for a baroque church of the martyrs in the centre of the arena (which would no doubt have echoed his work on that other great Catholic shrine of St Peter's) eventually came to nothing; the pope at the time, Clement X, settled instead for a wooden cross raised on the top of the building and his painted text commemorating the religious significance of the place. But by the eighteenth century, to the casual visitor, the Colosseum might well have seemed completely taken over by the Church. As well as the chapel, there was the cross in the middle of the arena, the landmark for so many of those nineteenth-century tourists (put up courtesy of Benedict XIV), and tabernacles of the Stations of the Cross around the arena's edge, commemorating the different stages of the Passion of Christ (illustration 2, p. 6). The place must also have been buzzing with religious personnel, from the orders of monks who serviced the shrines to the renowned local holy man who did good works in the city during the day and camped out in the Colosseum at night (he was later canonised as St Benedict Joseph Labre). Here was the place to listen to sermons, take communion, receive

26. One of the most famous recreations of the Colosseum was a late eighteenth-century cork model of the structure as it then stood. It included the small church that had been built at the arena's east end.

indulgences and tune in to the holiness of the martyrs. It was all a bit too much for some Protestant visitors. William Beckford, for example, the builder of the neo-Gothic extravaganza at Fonthill, had no time at all for the 'few lazy abbots' whom he found in the arena at their devotions: they 'would have made a lion's mouth water, fatter, I dare say, than any saint in the whole martyrology'.

But on a closer look the takeover of the arena by the Church was not quite so complete. It was challenged from two directions. On the one hand, the creeping Christianisation of the Colosseum had not entirely obliterated its early less pious uses. As late as the 1670s (just before Clement's cross went up on the top of the building) there was a proposal to hold another bullfight there, which was only just prevented through the efforts of a persistent cleric. Even in the eighteenth century it attracted some fairly rough trade. There is a story of how in 1742 the caretaker of the church in the arena was abducted and stabbed, and lost one of his hands (prompting Pope Benedict to close off much of the building). And, of course, the stinking pile of manure remained in the northern corridors long after the Stations of the Cross and all the rest had graced the arena.

On the other hand, as time went on, there came to be increasing pressure from a strictly archaeological lobby. Not that archaeologists could not be Christians, or vice versa. Just as there was no simple divide between despoilers of the building and Christians, so also there was an overlap between religious and archaeological activity: some of the most important early archaeological and restoration work on the Colosseum was sponsored by the popes. But from the nineteenth century on, we start to see a growing pressure to investigate the

27. The eastern end of the Colosseum is marked by the stark early-nineteenth-century buttress, which sealed the perimeter wall against further deterioration. In the foreground are the remaining ancient bollards that once circled the amphitheatre. In the background, the tents erected for staging the MTV Music awards which took place at the Colosseum in November 2004. The head of Rome's archaeological service objected to the monument being used in this way: 'debased, exploited, commercialised'. Unlike the ancient Colosseum?

ancient history of the monument without specific reference to the holy martyrs and to privilege archaeology over religion. To put it bluntly, if you wanted to find out what lay underneath the arena, the religious bric-à-brac littering its surface had to go.

ANTIQUARIANS AND ARCHAEOLOGISTS

The turning point in the archaeology (and with it the appearance) of the Colosseum came in the 1870s, with the first excavations of the site sponsored by the authorities of the new Italian state. There had been digging, on and off, in and around the monument for centuries, and those with an archaeological bent had repeatedly decried its plundering. In the fifteenth century, excavation revealed parts of its elaborate drainage system. There were some exploratory trenches dug in the early eighteenth century looking for the arena floor, as well as some wildly over-optimistic plans (which never came to anything) for a complete excavation and clearance of the site. Much more substantial work was carried out from the 1790s onwards, digging out the rubble from the corridors, and later (as we saw in Chapter 5) uncovering parts of the substructions beneath what we know to be the arena floor. But these were abandoned because of flooding and backfilled. Throughout the middle years of the nineteenth century clearance of unsafe elements went on, combined with more and more unashamed rebuilding. In the 1830s, for example, Pope Gregory XVI sponsored the reconstruction of a large part of what was missing on the south side – a section of eight arches put back as new in nineteenth-century brickwork. But none of this work significantly disturbed the essentially religious character of the monument. In fact an engraving of the excavations of the substructions shows the tabernacles of the Stations of the Cross still standing around the edge (endpapers); and the central cross was replaced when the hole was refilled.

That changed in the 1870s when, under State rather than Church sponsorship, substructions were uncovered again. This time the religious furniture of the arena was treated with no such delicacy: the Stations of the Cross were to be torn down, as was the central cross – and the then resident hermit (who had a picturesque hovel above the arena) was to be summarily evicted. It caused an outcry from many Catholics: 'pray-ins' were held in the arena in an attempt to stop the work proceeding and the Pope himself made his protests. But to no avail. Excavations started in 1874 – the archaeologist, Pietro Rosa, apparently using the threat of a 'moonlight masquerade' which had been planned for the Colosseum as an alibi for the work (better an excavation than the profanation of the sacred site with a carnival, or so his argument went). They got much further than the earlier excavators, revealing the complete depth of the substructions over most of the arena. But it was enormously expensive and once more drainage proved problematic. The hole flooded with water which soon stagnated and it was several years before it could be channelled out.

Rodolfo Lanciani, an archaeologist who wrote regular reports on archaeological news from Rome for the English magazine *The Athenaeum*, described the eventually successful draining in April 1879: 'The stagnant waters which inundated the substructions of the Coliseum were drained off some days ago amidst loud cheers from the crowd assembled to witness the ceremony.' But he goes on: 'Poor Coliseum! it was no longer recognisable since the upsetting of the arena by Signor Rosa in 1874.' Just over half of the basement area remained on display, while it was still possible to walk over the rest of the 'surface' of the arena, until that too was dug up in the 1930s. It is a sad irony that in the very year, 1878, that Henry James published his *Daisy Miller*, with its fatal moonlight tryst under the cross in the arena's centre, the cross was no more and large areas of the arena were submerged beneath pools of stagnant water.

Religion never fully returned to the Colosseum. From the 1870s it was increasingly established as a state monument and an archaeological site. Indeed when the Pope turns up on Good Friday, as he still does, to celebrate the Stations of the Cross, there is a very strong sense that the monument no longer counts as 'his', that religion is being allowed briefly to intrude into the secular world (much as when the Druids are admitted to Stonehenge for the summer solstice). That said, there is a strange twist to the tale of the relations of the Church and the archaeology of the site which goes back to the Fascist era.

Mussolini, predictably enough, given his enthusiasm for the archaeology of the ancient city of Rome, sponsored further major excavations of the substructions, completely revealing what had still been left covered in the 1870s. He also made the Colosseum one of the focal points of his vast new road, the Via del Impero ('Imperial Way'), as it was then called, leading to the Piazza Venezia and he entertained Hitler there on his state visit in 1938. Hitler was apparently entranced by the building, spent several hours in it (when the planned military parades were conveniently rained off) and

28. The Colosseum provided a proud backdrop to Mussolini's inauguration of the Via del Impero in 1932. In 1970 the closing scenes of Bertolucci's film, *The Conformist* – set on the day of Mussolini's death – used the arches of the Colosseum and the low-life that inhabited them as a symbol of the disintegration of the Fascist regime.

saw in its design a model for a mass gathering-place for his *Volk*. But, in addition to impressing fellow dictators, Mussolini was concerned to smooth over the potential anxieties of the Catholic Church. So at the north side of the Colosseum's arena, the Fascist regime put a new cross to replace the one removed in the 1870s. Underneath they placed four inscriptions in Latin. One carried the words of a hymn regularly sung on Good Friday. Another – matching the tone of Benedict's inscription (pp. 164–5) – recorded a rather euphemistic version of the removal of the eighteenth-century cross:

> *Where the old cross stood religiously placed by our ancestors in the Flavian Amphitheatre ... removed on account of the vicissitudes of time, this new one takes its place ... in the year of our Lord 1926.*

The two others recorded the date according to different conventions: the first noting it as the fifth year of the pontificate of Pope Pius XI (and the sixteen-hundredth anniversary of the rediscovery by Helena, the mother of the emperor Constantine, of the remains of the 'true cross' on which Christ had been crucified); the second noting it as the twenty-sixth year of the reign of King Victor Emmanuel II and the fourth year of Mussolini's dictatorship. Every political or religious option was covered, in other words.

Mussolini's cross still stands at the side of the Colosseum's arena. But the inscribed texts were smashed when Fascism fell. Their wording is known because it was published at the time – and also because archaeologists have recovered a few fragments of the stones themselves. That is the twist. It is a

29. Mussolini's cross still stands at the northern edge of the arena.

new stage in the complex balance of power between archaeology and religion in the arena over the last 500 years to find archaeology now devoting itself to the reconstruction of this religious monument of Mussolini.

BOTANISTS

It was not only the paraphernalia of religion that was removed when the archaeologists moved in to the arena in the 1870s. As *Murray's Handbook* observed in 1843, while regretting that there were no dried flowers on sale as souvenirs, one of the main claims to fame of the Colosseum had long been its flora. For whatever reason – because of the extraordinary micro-climate within its walls or, as some thought more fancifully, because of the seeds that fell out of the fur of the exotic animals displayed in the ancient arena – an enormous range of plants, including some extraordinary rarities, thrived for centuries in the building ruins. The first catalogue of these was published in 1643 as an appendix to a herbal by Domenico Panaroli, scientist, astronomer and professor of Botany and Anatomy at the University of Rome. He listed a total of 337 different species. A hundred and fifty years later in 1815, in a work entirely devoted to the 'plants growing wild in the Flavian amphitheatre', another Professor of Botany and keeper of the Botanical Garden on the Janiculan Hill in Rome, Antonio Sebastiani, listed a total of 261 species – the reduced number perhaps connected not so much with Sebastiani's lack of observational skills but with the major excavations and consolidation work on the monument that would have disturbed the flora in the early years of the nineteenth century.

The most impressive and lavish catalogue, however, was the work of an English doctor and amateur botanist from Sheffield, Richard Deakin. In 1855 he published *The Flora of the Colosseum*, a magnificently illustrated compendium of 420 different species (though modern scientists have pedantically reduced his total to 418). Deakin had a keen eye for the symbolic value of what he found. One of his specimens was a plant known as Christ's Thorn:

> *Few persons … will notice this plant flourishing upon the vast ruins of the Colosseum of Rome, without being moved to reflect upon the scenes that have taken place on the spot on which he stands, and remember the numbers of these holy men who bore witness to the truth of their belief in Jesus, and shed their blood before the thousands of Pagans assembled around, as a testimony, securing for themselves an eternal crown, without thorns, and to us those blessed truths, on which only we build our future hope of bliss, and derive our present peace and comfort.*

But if the pious doctor found botany readily compatible with the religious significance of the Colosseum, the same was not true for archaeology – which threatened the very existence of what he studied:

> *The collection of the plants and the species noted has been made some years; but since that time, many of the plants have been destroyed, from the alterations and restorations that have been made in the ruins; a circumstance that cannot but be lamented. To preserve a further falling of any portion is most desirable; but to carry the restorations, and the brushing and cleaning, to the extent to which it has been subjected, instead of leaving it in its*

Capparis spinosa.

30. Richard Deakin's *Flora of the Colosseum* illustrated many of the species to be found there. Here the caper plant sprouts from an antique column, adorned with its own imaginative foliage.

wild and solemn grandeur, is to destroy the impression and soli-tary lesson which so magnificent a ruin is calculated to make upon the mind.

Deakin died in 1873. There is a good chance that he lived long enough to hear of his nightmare coming true. For the first action of the new archaeological authorities in 1870 was the destruction not of the Stations of the Cross, but of what they would have called 'the weeds'. Today – despite some optimistic calculations by modern scientists which suggest that there are over 240 species still hanging on in the build-ing – the Colosseum is virtually a flower-free zone. One of the biggest items of expenditure in the maintenance budget is surely weedkiller.

Deakin's words must prompt us to reflect on how we want to experience our Wonders of the World and how the various competing claims to such international cultural symbols can ever be reconciled. It would be naive to imagine that we really should give the Colosseum over to the plants. If they had not been cleared in 1870, the building would now be – as any architect or conservationist will insist – close to collapse and we would have lost the monument, and its capacity to inspire, irretrievably. Common sense suggests that one should feel grateful that nature has been kept at bay and that the building is now well maintained, carefully studied, neat and tidy, and safe enough to host the occasional rock concert in a good cause. All the same it is hard not to feel slightly nostalgic for the romance of its ruins and for those parts of the building's history swept away in the pursuit of the archae-ology of the Roman amphitheatre. It is hard not to miss Deakin's anemones and pinks, not to mention the church, the blood of the martyrs, the moonlight walks, even the Roman fever ...

MAKING A VISIT?

AVOIDING THE QUEUE

Three million visitors a year puts a strain on the facilities and the infrastructure of almost any tourist site. There are queues to buy an entrance ticket to the Colosseum, even outside the peak summer season. We saw a fifteen-minute line at midday on one rainy Thursday in November – admittedly after the monument had been closed for most of the morning owing to a strike of custodians. There are various tricks, however, to avoid the worst of the waiting:

1. The traditional advice, for this and for other especially popular Italian museums and sites, is to turn up between fifteen and thirty minutes before the monument opens. But the truth is that many other visitors will have had the same idea. It is probably just as effective – even if it does not produce quite the same glow of virtue – to turn up at the end of the day, just before the ticket office closes, which is one hour before the site itself shuts.

2. It is now possible to book tickets in advance either by phone or on-line, or to buy a museum discount card which gives the holder access to a range of sites and museums in the

[182]

city of Rome cheaply and without having to queue at each site. Information on different methods of advance payment is available in English on the archaeological service's information line (currently +39 06 39967700) or on their website (www.archeorm.arti.beniculturali.it).

3. For those who do not want to plan in advance, the important thing to know is that (at the time of writing, at least – these arrangements do change periodically) the entrance ticket for the Colosseum also gives access to the nearby site of the Palatine, and vice versa. The canny visitor will buy their joint ticket at the Palatine ticket office, about five minutes' walk from the Colosseum, near the arch of Titus, where there is rarely a serious queue. Needless to say, the Palatine itself, with the remains of the Roman imperial palace, is also well worth a visit (despite Byron's unfavourable comparison with the ruins of the Colosseum, p. 4).

A GOOD LOOK AT THE OUTSIDE

The key thing to remember when visiting the Colosseum is that more than half the original outer wall has disappeared. The best way to take this in (and the building is horribly confusing if you do not) is to walk right around the circumference of the monument before you step inside. Starting at the west end, coming from the Via dei Fori Imperiali, you will see very clearly where the outer wall comes to an abrupt stop, with a nineteenth-century brick buttress that copies the original arcading. Walking around to the south, a line of white stones in the pavement marks where the original outer wall once ran; what now appears to be the outer wall on this side of the monument is in fact the wall of the second internal corridor (hence the stairs leading to the upper floors that are visible inside, and apparently blocking off, several of these 'outer' arches). The original perimeter wall picks up again at the east end, with another much more brutal nineteenth-century buttress, and continues unbroken around the northern side of the monument. On this surviving section, the numbers above the entrance arches are still visible, most distinctly towards the west end (numbers 51 to 54) where the stonework has been cleaned.

The outside of the Colosseum also reveals clearly – and much more clearly than the inside – the enormous scale of the interventions and restorations since antiquity. You do not need to be a trained archaeologist to spot many of the sections of modern infill, often in obviously modern brickwork. Besides, several of those who left their mark in the fabric of the building also advertised the fact with prominent inscriptions on its exterior. Pope Benedict's inscription (pp. 164–5), for example, can be seen above the main east door and just beneath it the head of Christ, the symbol of the Order of St Salvator, which once owned part of the monument. At the west entrance, Pope Pius IX placed a replica of Benedict's inscription, while adding a record of his own restoration in 1852.

It is also well worth exploring a little more widely beyond the monument itself. Towards the east are the five remaining bollards which once acted (we guess) as some kind of boundary marker or crowd control; immediately around them the Roman pavement surface has been preserved. Further in this direction, across the main road, lie the remains of one of the gladiatorial training camps, the Ludus Magnus (p. 136). The distinctive outline of part of its practice arena can be seen from the Via S. Giovanni in Laterano (in an excavation visible from the left-hand side of the street as you walk away from the Colosseum); the rest of the complex is still buried under the nearby modern buildings.

At the west end, the most impressive monument has no direct connection with the Colosseum. It is the arch dedicated in AD 315 in honour of the emperor Constantine. Less striking, but more closely related to the story of the amphitheatre, are the foundations of two other monuments. Closest to the Via dei Fori Imperiali is the roughly square base on which the Colossus itself stood from the early second century AD. Between that and the arch of Constantine are the now scanty remains of what was once a famous landmark, put up in the late first century AD by the emperor Domitian – presumably partly to leave his own mark near the amphitheatre of his father and brother (Vespasian and Titus). This was a monumental fountain, known as the Meta Sudans. Its central feature was conical in shape, like the turning post used for races in the circus (*meta*); *sudans* means that it 'sweated' or 'dripped' (see illustration 16, p. 95).

THE VIEW FROM INSIDE

The plan of the Colosseum may be simple, but it is nevertheless very easy to lose your bearings once inside (especially as the methods used to channel the crowds mean that you emerge into the arena itself some distance around the circumference from the point at which you entered the outer corridors of the monument). The best advice is to keep your eye on where the main outer wall is preserved (that is obvious from most parts of the building) and to remember that that is the north!

Visitors now have access to two floors of the monument only, the ground and first floors, and parts of both of these are regularly closed off to allow repair work. The first floor gives an excellent view of the whole structure (as well as offering wonderful vistas out over the surrounding area) and is the best place to start. Although this is less than half way up the original height of the monument, it is a steep climb up the stairs on a hot day. Most visitors prefer to use the lifts which have been neatly tucked in behind the nineteenth-century buttress at the east end. From the walkway around the edge of the arena at this level (which is just above the vault of the 'third corridor' on our cross-section, figure 3) you can look down into substructions beneath the level of the arena floor, which are not open to the public; and there is an excellent view of the reconstructed seating (which may help envisage the original appearance of the monument, even though it is in detail entirely wrong). Away from the arena's edge, near the entrance to the lifts, is a small display of material found in the building – balustrades from where the stairways came out into the seating area, late-Roman inscriptions designating the occupants of particular sections of the elite seating and some vivid graffiti (illustration 17, p. 97) – plus some puzzling models of the machinery used to bring the animals up from the basements. Much of the space of the outer corridors on the north side is now usually given over to temporary exhibitions.

The ground floor is rather more confusing: parts of it (including sometimes even the section of wooden flooring built to replicate the original arena floor) are often closed to visitors; many of the vaults are used as deposits for quantities of stray masonry from the original structure. But there are also more details to look at here than on the first floor, especially near the north and south entrances. At the north, Mussolini's cross (pp. 175–6) still stands at the arena's edge and on the vault of one of the main passages leading into the building (immediately to the left of the central entranceway) is the best surviving piece of the stucco decoration that would once have adorned much of the structure. In the main south entrance, which originally led to the imperial box, have been placed two inscriptions celebrating one of the late-Roman repairs to the building. Moving towards the arena, the start of the so-called 'passageway of Commodus' (p. 134) is visible on the right. Away from the arena itself, in the corridor between the south and west entrances, is the tantalising shape of a crucifix in the wall: nothing to do with Christians, but the setting for one of the fountains that serviced the building.

AMENITIES

There are far fewer fountains and other services in the building now than there were in antiquity: no café and the queues for the (few) lavatories sometimes almost equal those at the ticket office. There is, however, an excellent book and souvenir shop on the first floor, and another smaller one on the ground. For refreshments, the modern 'gladiators' usually make for the stand-up coffee bar in the adjacent Metro station (it is a strangely picturesque sight to watch them mingling with the commuters, helmets on the counter). For anything more substantial, or for a seat, the restaurants and cafés nearest to the Colosseum are best avoided, over-priced and decidedly uninspiring in cuisine. Better fare is to be had as you walk down the Via S Giovanni in Laterano and the Via Santi Quattri Coronati to the east; or, a little further away to the west, up the Via della Madonna dei Monti off the Via dei Fori Imperiali, turning right at the Hotel Forum ... whose famous roof terrace is reputed to be the setting for the conversation between Mrs Slade and Mrs Ansley in Edith Wharton's 'Roman Fever' (p. 10).

FURTHER READING

GENERAL AND INTRODUCTORY

The most comprehensive recent introduction to all aspects of
the Colosseum is A. Gabucci (ed.), *The Colosseum* (Getty
Museum, Los Angeles, 2001), though be warned that the
English translation of the original Italian edition (Milan,
2000) is sometimes inaccurate and occasionally misleading.
Also useful are P. Connolly, *Colosseum: Rome's Arena of Death*
(London, 2003) – especially good for its careful reconstruction drawings and its explanations of the basement areas; L.
Abbondanza, *The Valley of the Colosseum* (Rome, 1997), the
site-guide produced by the Italian archaeological service, but
widely available; and P. Quennell, *The Colosseum* (New York,
1971), which is excellent on the medieval and later history of
the building (though sadly out of print). Other important
studies, available only in Italian, include M. L. Conforto et
al., *Anfiteatro Flavio: immagine, testimonianze, spettacoli*
(Rome, 1988), and R. Rea, *Rota Colisei* (Milan, 2002).

Amphitheatres in general are the subject of D. L-
Bomgardner, *The Story of the Roman Amphitheatre* (London,
2000), and of an important new book by K. Welch, *The
Roman Amphitheatre from its Origins to the Colosseum*
(Cambridge, 2005). The main work of reference on

amphitheatres is the two-volume study by J.-C. Golvin, *L'Amphithéâtre Romain: essai sur la théorisation de sa forme et de ses fonctions* (Paris, 1988), but note that a printing error on Golvin's definitive plan of the Colosseum reversed the points of the compass, marking south as north. This error has crept into later books (including Bomgardner's), causing considerable confusion.

There has been an enormous amount of recent writing on gladiators and other forms of Roman spectacle (some, but not all, prompted by the movie *Gladiator*). Particularly influential have been K. Hopkins' chapter 'Murderous Games', in his *Death and Renewal* (Cambridge, 1983), and C. Barton, *Sorrows of the Ancient Romans: the gladiator and the monster* (Princeton, 1993). Good general surveys of the phenomenon include R. Auguet, *Cruelty and Civilization: the Roman games* (London, 1972); D. Kyle, *Spectacles and Death in Ancient Rome* (London, 1998); and T. Wiedemann, *Emperors and Gladiators* (London & New York, 1992). G. Ville, *La Gladiature en occident des origines à la mort de Domitien* (Rome, 1981) is a rigorously detailed account. Two exhibition catalogues provide useful illustration of the material evidence (including surviving gladiatorial armour): E. Köhne and C. Ewigleben (eds.), *Gladiators and Caesars* (London, 2000) and – a magnificently illustrated book, though only available in Italian – A. La Regina (ed.), *Sangue e arena* (Milan, 2001). M. M. Winkler (ed.), *Gladiator: film and history* (Malden, MA, & Oxford, 2004) is a lively collection of essays on modern popular representation of gladiators and the ancient context.

The Cambridge Illustrated History of the Roman World, edited by G. Woolf (Cambridge, 2003), is an excellent, up-to-the-minute introduction to the historical and cultural background of the Colosseum. The best on-site guide to the ancient monuments of the city of Rome is A. Claridge, *Rome: an Oxford archaeological guide* (Oxford, 1998).

ANCIENT TEXTS

The main ancient texts which underpin our account of gladiatorial shows and the world of the Colosseum are:

Cassius Dio, *Roman History* (a narrative – now surviving only in parts – written in Greek in the third century AD, covering Rome's history from its foundation to the writer's own lifetime)

Martial, *The Book of the Shows* (or *On Spectacles*, as it is often called, a collection of poetry written to celebrate the opening of the Colosseum in AD 80)

Pliny (the Elder), *Natural History* (a vast encyclopaedia of the natural world, written in the mid first century AD)

'Scriptores Historiae Augustae' (a mysterious – and often unbelievably lurid – collection of lives of emperors and usurpers from Hadrian to the end of the third century AD, probably written at the end of the fourth; usually abbreviated as SHA)

Suetonius, *Lives of the Caesars* (a series of twelve biographies of Roman dictators and emperors from Julius Caesar to Domitian, written in the early second century AD)

Tacitus, *Annals* (an account of Roman history from the death of the first emperor Augustus probably – though the end does not survive – to the death of Nero, written in the early second century AD)

Translations of all these – and most other classical writers we have referred to – are available in the Loeb Classical Library. Reliable English versions of Suetonius and Tacitus (and of portions of Dio, Pliny and SHA) are also to be found in the Penguin Classics series. A selection of Martial's verses from *The Book of the Shows* is included in the Penguin Classics volume *Martial in English* (eds. J. P. Sullivan and A. J. Boyle).

CHAPTER I

Nineteenth-century tourism to Rome, as well as literary and artistic responses, are acutely discussed in C. Edwards (ed.), *Roman Presences: receptions of Rome in European culture, 1789–1945* (Cambridge, 1999); the chapters by C. Chard and J. Lyon are especially relevant. The appeal of the mid-nine-teenth-century Colosseum is captured by C. Woodward, *In Ruins* (London, 2001), Chapter 1, 'Who Killed Daisy Miller?', and (with an American focus) W. L. Vance, *America's Rome* (New Haven & London, 1989), Volume 1, Chapter 2 ('The Colosseum: ambiguities of empire'). Amongst an enormous bibliography which explores more generally the northern European engagement with Italy and the Mediterranean, note J. Pemble, *The Mediterranean Passion: Victorians and Edwardians in the South* (Oxford, 1987); M. Liversidge and C. Edwards, *Imagining Rome: British artists and Rome in the nineteenth century* (London,

1996); and C. Hornsby (ed.), *The Impact of Italy: the Grand Tour and beyond* (London, British School at Rome, 2000).

In addition to the literary references sourced in the text, Charles Dickens' effusion on the Colosseum is from his *Pictures from Italy* (London, 1846) and Byron's famous lines in *Childe Harold's Pilgrimage* are from Canto IV.

CHAPTER 2

The Colosseum's ancient literary fame depends heavily on Martial's poems in *The Book of the Shows*, discussed by W. Fitzgerald in *Martial: the heterogeneous world* (Chicago, forthcoming) and soon to be the subject of a definitive commentary by K. Coleman (Oxford, 2006). The reactions of the emperor Constantius to the city can be found in Book 16 of Ammianus' multi-volume history of Rome (translated in the Loeb Classical Library and Penguin Classics). The archaeological impact of the building is straightforwardly reviewed in Bomgardner's *Story of the Roman Amphitheatre*. The description of El Jem as a 'shrunken Colosseum' is from an architectural study by M. Wilson-Jones, 'Designing amphitheatres', in *Mitteilungen des Deutschen Archaelogischen Instituts (Römische Abteilung)*, 100 (1993). Amphitheatres in Britain include a newly discovered example in London, which is explored in N. Bateman, *Gladiators at the Guildhall: the story of London's Roman amphitheatre and medieval Guildhall* (London, 2002).

The story of the Golden House and the end of Nero's reign are covered in two good biographies of Nero: M. Griffin, *Nero: the end of a dynasty* (London, 1984), and E. Champlin, *Nero* (Cambridge, MA, & London, 2003). The main Roman account of the rise of Vespasian is in Tacitus' *Histories* (covering a later period than his *Annals*); the Talmudic story of the flea is in Masechet Gittin (56b–57a). The triumphal procession of Vespasian and Titus is described in Book 7 of Josephus' *Jewish War* and is the subject of M. Beard, 'The Triumph of Flavius Josephus', in A. J. Boyle and W. J. Dominik (eds.), *Flavian Rome: culture, image, text* (Leiden & Boston, 2003). The Colossus is discussed in S. Carey, *Pliny's Catalogue of Culture: art and empire in the Natural History* (Oxford, 2003). The squib about Veii is reported in Suetonius' *Life of Nero*. The full technical study of the dedicatory inscription is in German by G. Alföldy, in *Zeitschrift für Papyrologie und Epigraphik*, 109 (1995). The 'Bede' quotation is from a miscellany known as the *Collectanea*, edited and translated by M. Bayless, M. Lapidge et al. (Dublin, 1988); attributed to him in the sixteenth century, it is almost certainly nothing to do with Bede at all – though it is nevertheless probably of early medieval date.

The pre-Colosseum history of the amphitheatre is now expertly explored by K. Welch in *The Roman Amphitheatre*. Caligula's disdain for the monument of the aristocrat (one Statilius Taurus) is reported in Book 59 of Dio's *History*. The amazed rustics are a creation of the poet Calpurnius Siculus, whose Eclogues are translated in *Minor Latin Poets* (Loeb Classical Library); Eclogue 7 spotlights the amphitheatre. The political analysis presented in this chapter draws on the discussion in Hopkins, *Death and Renewal* (Chapters 2 and 3). Other, differently nuanced, accounts of the political shifts in Rome over this period include J. R. Patterson, *Political Life in the City of Rome* (London, 2000), a very useful review, primarily intended for students, and T. P. Wiseman, *Roman*

Political Life 90 BC–AD 69 (Exeter, 1985). Those shifts are also the theme of R. Syme's classic, *The Roman Revolution* (Oxford, 1939), written in the shadow of the European dictatorships of the 1930s. Ancient Chinese reactions to Rome are collected in F. Hirth, *China and the Roman Orient: researches into their ancient and medieval relations as represented in old Chinese records* (Leipzig, 1885).

CHAPTERS 3 AND 4

The varied displays in the arena (including several of the acts lauded by Martial) are the subject of influential essays by K. Coleman, 'Fatal Charades: Roman executions staged as mythological enactments', *Journal of Roman Studies*, 80 (1990) and 'Launching into History: aquatic displays in the early empire', *Journal of Roman Studies*, 83 (1993). The translation we have used of the Laureolus/Prometheus verse is by F. Ahl, from another collection of translations of Martial, *Epigrams of Martial, Englished by divers hands* (Berkeley & London, 1987) (eds. J. P. Sullivan and P. Whigham). Tertullian's main attack on such displays is to be found in his *De Spectaculis* (*On the Shows*).

Most discussions of 'what happened' at gladiatorial shows rely on a few key texts in addition to Martial: notably, Seneca's *Letter 7*, describing the lunchtime executions; the *Passion of SS Perpetua and Felicity* (not available in either Loeb or Penguin translations, but there are several English versions – for example in H. Musurillo (ed.), *The Acts of the Christian Martyrs: introduction, texts and translations* (Oxford, 1972), and R. Valantasis (ed.), *Religions of Late Antiquity in Practice* (Princeton, 2000)); and Dio's descriptions of the emperor

Commodus' antics in the arena in Book 73 of his *History* (on which, see Chapter 4 of O. Hekster, *Commodus: an emperor at the crossroads* (Amsterdam, 2002)). Less often used is the rhetorical exercise on the gladiatorial theme – one of the Declamations once (wrongly) believed to have been written by the Roman oratorical theorist Quintilian, now translated in L. A. Sussman (ed.), *The Major Declamations Ascribed to Quintilian: a translation* (Frankfurt etc., 1987). But much of the ancient evidence for the activities in the arena is scattered, fragmentary, untranslated and hard to track down outside a major research library. Other literary texts we have referred to are: the *Letters* of Symmachus, esp. nos. 2, 46 and 10, 8 & 9 (translated into French in the Budé series); Olympiodorus (41.2, on Symmachus' expenditure), translated in R. C. Blockley (ed.), *Fragmentary Classicizing Historians of the later Roman Empire*, Volume 2 (Liverpool, 1983); Seneca, *Letter* 70 (on the suicide of the Germans); Plutarch's essay *A Pleasant Life is Impossible following the precepts of Epicurus* (for his aside, Chapter 17, on the gladiators' last meal); and, on the same subject, an aside in another tract of Tertullian, the *Apologeticus* (Chapter 42). The late-Roman figures for seating capacity are taken from the so-called *Regionary Catalogues* (*Notitia Urbis Romae* – for which there is no easily available English translation). Galen's career with gladiators is discussed by J. Scarborough, 'Galen and the Gladiators', in *Episteme*, 5 (1971).

Our calculations of gladiatorial numbers and death rates, as well as our reconstruction of other aspects of the world of the arena, depend heavily on the evidence of inscriptions. Text and translation of the decree regulating expenditure under Marcus Aurelius can be found in J. H. Oliver and R. E.

A. Palmer, 'Minutes of an Act of the Roman Senate', *Hesperia*, 24 (1955) with further discussion by M. Carter in *Phoenix*, 57 (2003). Gladiatorial graffiti from Pompeii is conveniently collected in L. Jacobelli, *Gladiators at Pompeii* (Rome, 2003). The calendar of Trajan's celebrations is published (untranslated) in A. Degrassi, *Inscriptiones Italiae* 13, 1 (Rome, 1947); Glauco can be found in the vast multi-volume collection of Roman inscriptions, the *Corpus Inscriptionum Latinarum*, Volume 5, 3466; and the Thracian in Volume 6, 10194. The best text of the seating arrangements of the Arvals in the arena is in J. Scheid, *Commentarii Fratrum Arvalium quae supersunt* (Rome, 1998), Document 48 (with French translation). The death of eleven gladiators out of eleven pairs is recorded in the *Corpus*, volume 10, 6012.

The idea of the gladiatorial spectacles as 'political theatre' is a major theme of Hopkins' 'Murderous Games', in *Death and Renewal*. The simplicity of that model is effectively challenged by J. Edmondson, 'Dynamic Arenas', in W. J. Slater (ed.), *Roman Theater and Society: E. Togo Salmon papers* 1 (Ann Arbor, 1996) – a notably acute study whose approach we have generally followed here. The '*infamia*' of gladiators is explored by C. Edwards in 'Unspeakable Professions', in J. P. Hallett and M. B. Skinner (eds.), *Roman Sexualities* (Princeton, 1997). The insult 'gladiator' is used more than once by Cicero of his enemy Mark Antony in his remarkable series of political invectives known as the *Philippics*; the ghastly possibility that a dead son might have ended up as a gladiator is raised by Seneca in his *Letter* 99; prohibitions on the elite becoming gladiators are discussed by B. Levick in 'The Senatus Consultum from Larinum', *Journal of Roman Studies*, 73 (1983). The bizarre custom involving the bride's hair is mentioned in the Roman dictionary of Festus, *De Significatione Verborum* (ed. W. Lindsay), 55.

The sexuality and glamour of the gladiator is discussed (with emphasis on the power of 'visuality') by E. Gunderson in 'The Ideology of the Arena', *Classical Antiquity*, 15 (1996), as well as in Edwards' 'Unspeakable Professions' (whence the phrase 'all sword') and in Barton's *Sorrows of the Ancient Romans* (the source of our quotation about the *tintinnabulum* from Herculaneum). One famous nineteenth-century version of the arena's high charge is expertly dissected by E. Prettejohn in '"The Monstrous Diversion of a Show of Gladiators": Simeon Solomon's *Habet!*' in Edwards (ed.), *Roman Presences*. The classic passage of Juvenal is from his sixth *Satire* (here translated by Peter Green); the lurid story of Faustina and the gladiator is told in the SHA biography of Marcus Antoninus (i.e. Aurelius); the pick-up of Sulla is described in Plutarch's *Life of Sulla*. Appropriate cold water is poured on the story of the rich lady in the gladiators' barracks by P. G. Guzzo (ed.), *Stories from an Eruption: Pompeii, Herculaneum and Oplontis* (Milan, 2003).

All aspects of procuring animals for the Colosseum are discussed by R. Wilson, *Animals for the Arena: the Roman wild beast trade* (Oxford, forthcoming), the role of the military is discussed by C. Epplett, 'The Capture of Animals by the Roman military' in *Greece and Rome*, 48 (2001). The idea of the star rhinoceros is floated in Ville, *La gladiature*, p. 149. Pompey's unfortunate experience with his elephants is recounted in Book 7 of Pliny's *Natural History*. The story of the London hippo Obaysch is told by N. J. Root, 'Victorian England's Hippomania', *Natural History*, 102 (1993). The letter of Ignatius to the Romans is translated in

Volume 1 of the Loeb translation of *The Apostolic Fathers*. The phenomenon of martyrdom and 'Martyr Acts' has been widely discussed recently: for different approaches, see G. W. Bowersock, *Martyrdom and Rome* (Cambridge, 1995); D. Boyarin, 'Martyrdom and the Making of Christianity and Judaism', *Journal of Early Christian Studies*, 6 (1998); and K. Hopkins, *A World Full of Gods* (London, 1999), Chapter 3.

The Greek historian speculating on the Etruscan origin of gladiators is Nicolaus of Damascus, who is quoted in Athenaeus' extraordinary compendium *Deipnosophistae* (*Philosophers at Dinner*), Book 4, 153f–154a.

CHAPTER 5

The effects of the fire in 217 are discussed by L. Lancaster, 'Reconstructing the Colosseum's Restorations after the Fire of 217', *Journal of Roman Archaeology*, 11 (1998), with some salutary remarks on the general difficulties of dating individual parts of the structure. The drawings of the stucco are fully illustrated in N. Dacos, 'Les stucs du Colisée', *Latomus*, 21 (1962); the graffito that is supposed to show the balustrading around the arena is in Connolly, *Colosseum*, p. 195. The classic study of the safety arrangements is A. Scobie, 'Spectator Security and Comfort at Gladiatorial Games', *Nikephoros*, 1 (1988).

The nineteenth-century debates about the substructures of the Colosseum and the question of naval battles are clearly explained by R. T. Ridley, *The Eagle and the Spade: archaeology in Rome during the Napoleonic era* (Cambridge, 1992), a full study of Roman archaeology during that period. There has been an enormous amount of recent work on the underground areas of the building, the drainage, foundations and the arrangements for the arena floor. The work of the German archaeologist H.-J. Beste has been crucial, though little of this is available in English. A flavour of his work can be found in his 'The Construction and Phases of Development of the Wooden Arena Flooring of the Colosseum', *Journal of Roman Archaeology*, 13 (2000); the same volume includes a review by R. Rea of recent archaeological work in and around the Colosseum ('Studying the Valley of the Colosseum (1970–2000): achievements and prospects'). Other detailed studies include D. Mertens et al., 'Il Colosseo. Lo studio degli "ipogei"', and H.-J. Beste, 'Neue Forschungsergebnisse zu einem Aufzugssystem im Untergeschoss des Kolosseums', *Mitteilungen des deutschen archaelogischen Instituts (Römische Abteilung)*, 105 (1998) and 106 (1999).

The methods of amphitheatre design are analysed in minute detail by Wilson-Jones in 'Designing Amphitheatres' (and, more generally, in his *Principles of Roman Architecture* (New Haven & London, 2000)); building processes are discussed by R. Taylor in *Roman Builders: a study in architectural process* (Cambridge, 2003) – chapter 4 is specifically concerned with the Colosseum. Other reflections are offered by L. Haselberger in 'Architectural Likenesses: models and plans of architecture in classical antiquity', *Journal of Roman Archaeology*, 10 (1997). The story of Hadrian and Apollodorus is told in Book 69 of Dio's *History*.

CHAPTER 6

A dazzling variety of post-antique uses of, and responses to, the Colosseum are collected in M. di Macco, *Il Colosseo: funzione simbolica, storica, urbana* (Rome, 1971). *The Wonders of Rome* is translated by F. M. Nichols (second edn, New York, 1986) and Master Gregory's *Wonders* by J. L. Osborne (Toronto, 1987).

The best specialist studies of the Colosseum in late antiquity are not in English: see, for example, G. Ville, 'Les Jeux de gladiateurs dans l'empire chrétien', *Mélanges de l'Ecole Française de Rome*, 72 (1960); T. Wiedemann, 'Das Ende der römischen Gladiatorenspiele', *Nikephoros*, 8 (1995); and S. Orlandi, 'Il Colosseo nel V secolo', in W. V. Harris (ed.), *The Transformations of urbs Roma in late antiquity* (*Journal of Roman Archaeology*, Supplement, 33 (1999)). The inscription from Spello is found (untranslated) in the *Corpus Inscriptionum Latinarum*, Volume II, 5265. For the late antique city of Rome more generally, see P. Llewellyn, *Rome in the Dark Ages* (London, 1971); B. Ward-Perkins, *From Classical Antiquity to the Middle Ages: urban public building in northern and central Italy AD 300–850* (Oxford, 1984); and, taking the story up to the fourteenth century (with lavish illustrations), R. Krautheimer, *Rome: profile of a city 312–1308* (Princeton, 1980).

The Renaissance architectural fascination with the Colosseum is briefly discussed, in the context of a clear discussion of the architectural orders, by J. Summerson, *The Classical Language of Architecture* (revised edition, London, 1980). Note also the detailed Italian study by F. Scoppola, 'Il Colosseo come modello …', in *Frondose Arcate: il Colosseo prima dell'archeologia* (Exhibition Catalogue, Palazzo Altemps, Rome, 2000). Good basic introductions to the architecture of the Renaissance can be found in the Pelican

History of Art series: L. H. Heydenreich and P. Davies, *Architecture in Italy, 1400–1500* (New Haven & London, 1996), and W. Lotz and D. Howard, *Architecture in Italy, 1500–1600* (New Haven & London, 1995). The 'borrowings' from the Roman amphitheatre in the London Coliseum are described in F. Barker, *The House that Stoll Built: the story of the Coliseum Theatre* (London, 1957). Poggio's lament is from his *De Varietate Fortunae* (1448; a modern text and edition by O. Merisalo was published in Helsinki, 1993); it was famously quoted in Chapter 71 of Edward Gibbon's *The Decline and Fall of the Roman Empire* which includes a withering account of the Colosseum's post-antique history, including such events as the fourteenth-century bullfight.

After more than a century, the definitively sceptical analysis of the evidence for martyrdom in the Colosseum (and one written from within the Catholic church) is still H. Delehaye, 'L'Amphithéâtre flavien et ses environs dans les textes hagiographiques', *Analecta Bollandiana*, 16 (1897). William Beckford's barbs on the lazy abbots are originally from Letter 22 of his *Dreams, Waking Thoughts and Incident*, originally published in 1783, suppressed, republished as part of his *Italy: with sketches of Spain and Portugal* (London, 1834) and now available in an edition by R. J. Gemmett (Rutherford, NJ, 1972). The silver gilt image of St Peter is illustrated in Di Macco, *Il Colosseo*.

Lanciani's reports are conveniently reprinted in A. L. Cubberley (ed.), *Notes from Rome by Rodolfo Lanciani* (London, 1988); the general archaeological atmosphere of Rome in the 1870s and 80s is captured by R. Lanciani, *Ancient Rome in the Light of Recent Discoveries* (Rome, 1888) – discussed by M. Beard, 'Archaeology and Collecting in

Late Nineteenth-Century Rome', in *Ancient Art to Post Impressionism: masterpieces from the Ny Carlsberg Glyptotek, Copenhagen* (Exhibition Catalogue, Royal Academy of Arts, London, 2004). Hitler's enthusiasm for the Colosseum and the designs for buildings based on it are documented in A. Scobie, *Hitler's State Architecture: the impact of classical antiquity* (University Park, PA, & London, 1990). The history of Mussolini's Via del Impero (now, dei Fori Imperiali) is vividly illustrated and documented in L. Barroero et al., *Via dei Fori Imperiali. La zona archeologica di Roma: urbanistica, beni artistici e politica culturale* (Venice, 1983).

The history of the Colosseum's role in botany is exhaustively discussed (in Italian) in G. Caneva (ed.), *Amphitheatrum Naturae. Il Colosseo: storia e ambiente letti attraverso la sua flora* (Milan, 2004).

LIST OF ILLUSTRATIONS

LIST OF FIGURES BY TOM CROSS

While every effort has been made to contact copyright-holders of
illustrations, the author and publishers would be grateful for information about any illustrations where they have been unable to trace them,
and would be glad to make amendments in further editions.

ACKNOWLEDGEMENTS

Collaboration comes in many forms. Keith and I had often dreamed up plans to write a book together. It is a sad irony that this, our only joint venture, is the product of a strange form of collaboration in which one of the parties is no longer around to share the fun – or the blame. When Keith died in March 2004, he had already done a considerable amount of work towards a book on the Colosseum, which I agreed to continue and complete. Despite the circumstances, over the last six months, I have tremendously enjoyed the debates and dialogues I have had with him, through his notes and rough drafts.

In the process, many of our friends have lent a hand: in particular, Nigel Cassidy, Chloe Chard, Robin Cormack, William Harris, Henry Hurst, Christopher Kelly, Martin Millett, Helen Morales, Hilary Perrott, Walter Scheidel, Andrew Wallace-Hadrill and Sophia Whitbread. The staff of the British School at Rome expertly arranged permits to visit 'closed' areas of the Colosseum, provided a marvellous Roman library and an agreeable base in the city. Peter Foskett of The Daniel Connal Partnership (Colchester office) kindly tackled the provisional cost of the Colosseum's foundations – despite our unusual and amateur specification. At Profile, Peter Carson, Penny Daniel, Andrew Franklin, Trevor

Horwood and Amelia Rowland made light work of the final
stages of writing, editing and publication.

MB
November 2004

INDEX

WONDERS OF THE WORLD

This is a small series of books, under the general editorship of Mary Beard, that will focus on some of the world's most famous sites or monuments.

Already available

Mary Beard: *The Parthenon*
Robert Irwin: *The Alhambra*
Richard Jenkyns: *Westminster Abbey*
Simon Goldhill: *The Temple of Jerusalem*